Spread Your Wings & Fly

Spread Your Wings & Fly

9 Secrets to Create A Magical Life Through Small Steps

NINU BALAN KAILATH

Dedication

To my husband, for your endless love, continuous support, and unwavering faith in me; you're my forever and always.

To my family, for always grounding me and motivating me to fly higher; you are my wings and roots.

To my friends, for the shared laughs and smiles, genuine feedback, and the little nudges that kept me rolling.

This book is a mirror of the love, strength, and inspiration I have been blessed to receive from all of you.

I love you dearly and forever!

Contents

Dedication --- 5
Contents --- 7
Acknowledgements --- 9
Introduction --- 11

1: THE POWER OF DAILY HABIT --- 15
Building a Powerful Daily Routine --- 16
How Habits Evolve --- 20
Activity: My Habits - Worksheet --- 22
Habit Formation and Tracking --- 25
Effective Planning and Task Management --- 35
Final Thoughts --- 37
Key Points to Remember --- 39

2: THE ULTIMATE SELF-UPGRADE --- 41
Discovering Your Core Values --- 42
Activity: Values Clarification Exercise --- 44
Creating A Vision Board --- 46
Creating a Bucket List --- 49
The 101 Life Goals --- 55
Embracing a Positive Mindset --- 59
Prompts for Positive Mindset --- 65
Key Points to Remember --- 67

3: PATHWAYS TO MENTAL WELLNESS --- 69
Meditation --- 70
Affirmations --- 79
Activity: Create Your Own Affirmations --- 79
Visualization --- 82
Journaling Practices --- 86
Reconnecting with Nature --- 94
Digital Detox and Mindful Technology Use --- 96
Key Points to Remember --- 99

4: MASTERING HEALTH AND FITNESS --- 101
Importance of Active Living --- 102
Activity: Create your own Active Living Plan --- 105
Understanding the "Plateaus" --- 106
The Importance of Breaks --- 108
Healthy Eating --- 111
The Importance of Sleep and Recovery --- 113
Key Points to Remember --- 116

5: CREATING A HARMONIOUS HOME --- 117
Keeping Your Home Clean and Organised --- 119
Activity: 30-Day Decluttering Challenge --- 125
Making Space for New Things --- 127
Boost Ambiance with Positive Elements --- 127
Create Functional Spaces --- 133

Maintaining a Harmonious Home --- 134
Key Points to Remember --- 136

6: CULTIVATING WEALTH MINDSET --- 137
Shifting Your Money Mindset --- 138
Steps To Overcome Money Energy Block --- 142
Activity: Transform Your Money Mindset --- 144
Budgeting Fundamentals --- 148
Expense Management --- 152
Debt Management Strategies --- 154
Financial Goal Setting --- 158
Building Multiple Income Streams --- 160
Activity: Passive Income Ideas --- 161
Financial Education and Literacy --- 166
Key Points to Remember --- 167

7: EMBRACING SUSTAINABLE LIVING --- 169
Reduce Plastic Consumption --- 171
Activity: Plastic Audit Challenge --- 172
Waste Management at Home --- 173
Growing Your Own Food --- 177
Water Conservation Strategies --- 179
Sustainable Energy Use --- 181
Activity: Home Energy Audit --- 184
Key Points to Remember --- 185

8: TURNING MILES INTO MEMORIES --- 187
Planning Trips with Purpose --- 189
Activity: Travel Vision Board --- 191
Balancing Local, Domestic, and International Travel --- 193
Taking a Sabbatical --- 197
Incorporating Travel Into Your Lifestyle --- 201
Activity: Travel Integration Roadmap --- 201
Capture and Preserve Travel Memories --- 202
Key Points to Remember --- 203

9: BUILDING STRONGER AND HEALTHIER RELATIONSHIPS --- 205
Cultivate Friendships --- 206
Activity: Reconnect With Your Friends --- 208
Maintain a Healthy Romantic Relationship --- 208
Nurturing Family Connections --- 213
Activity: Family Connection Calendar --- 220
Unplug to Reconnect --- 220
Other Thoughts --- 224
Key Points to Remember --- 226

Tools and Resources --- 227

Acknowledgements

With a heart full of gratitude, I dedicate this space to honour the people, experiences, and spiritual connections that have shaped my journey.

First and foremost, I extend my deepest thanks to my spiritual team—my angels, spirit guides, masters, and the universe. Their unwavering guidance, healing, and the signs they've provided have been the compass of my life. Without their support, this journey would not have been possible.

To my husband, my rock and partner in the beautiful fairytale life we've built together—thank you. Your love and support have been my strength, and together we've reached for the stars and grown in ways I never imagined. I am forever grateful to you for making life so magical and fulfilling.

To my parents, my heroes, I owe my deepest gratitude. You have shown me the power of perseverance, dedication, and truth. Through your example, I have learned to face failures with courage and setbacks with resilience. Your guidance has shaped me into the person I am today, and for that, I am eternally thankful.

To my Amma and Mama, who were like parents to me, your selfless love has been nothing short of amazing. Thank you for always being with me, guiding me, and showering me with love. Though you are no longer here, your presence continues to inspire and comfort me.

To my sisters, in-laws, niece, nephew, and every member of my extended family, thank you for your encouragement, kindness, and constant presence in my life. Each of you has contributed to my journey in unique and meaningful ways, filling my world with love, laughter, and inspiration.

To my friends, thank you for being the light in my life when I needed it most. You accepted me for who I truly am, allowing me to show my vulnerabilities without fear of judgment. The open feedback, the fun, and the joy of our catch-ups have been priceless. Your unwavering support and genuine connection have been a true gift, and this book is a testament to the love and strength you've brought into my life.

A special thank you to my editor, Alisha, for your patience and dedication. Your keen eye and thoughtful suggestions have been invaluable, and I am profoundly grateful for your role in bringing this book to life. Additionally, thank you to M.J Services for their exceptional work in formatting my book. Your expertise has made the final product truly shine!

Lastly, to everyone who has been a part of my journey—those who stayed and those who left—thank you. Each of you has left a mark on my life, and I am grateful for the lessons and the memories.

This book is a testament to the love, guidance, and support I've received from all of you.

Introduction

I'm a dreamer—a believer in the endless possibilities life has to offer. But dreams alone aren't enough. At some point, we all confront fears, doubts, and insecurities that hold us back. These struggles shape how we perceive ourselves, and this self-image becomes the foundation of everything we do. If you believe you're not good enough, your actions will reflect that narrative. But what if you could rewrite the story you tell yourself?

My journey has been far from easy. As a teenager, I faced academic struggles that shattered my confidence. Backlogs piled up, and there were moments when I felt completely incapable—like the time I scored 2 out of 100 in a subject. I labelled myself a failure, and that self-image seeped into every part of my life. My relationships didn't flourish, my dreams felt unattainable, and nothing seemed to fall into place. For years, I carried the weight of self-doubt, convinced that life would always be this way.

But one day, something changed. I realised this wasn't the life I wanted for myself. I wanted more. I wanted to rewrite my story. So I started from scratch, moving to Australia to pursue my Master's degree. That decision was a turning point. I worked hard, achieved high scores, and regained the confidence I had lost. Slowly but surely, I began achieving things I once thought were impossible. My mindset shifted, my energy transformed, and my life started to blossom.

Today, I'm living a life I once only dreamed of—a life full of joy, growth, and purpose. That doesn't mean I haven't faced failures or setbacks; I've had plenty. But I've learned to see them as stepping stones rather than barriers. By focusing on the positives, learning from my mistakes, and continually working on myself, I've built a balanced, meaningful, and fulfilling life.

This book is for anyone who feels stuck, who dreams of a better life but doesn't know where to begin. Through my journey, I'll show you how small changes can create magical transformations. Together, we'll explore ways to shift your energy, reshape your mindset, and unlock the power within you. Each chapter will guide you through practical steps to elevate every aspect of your life—your relationships, career, health, wealth, and more.

If I can transform my life, so can you. Believe in the magic of possibilities, and let's embark on this journey of transformation together.

Let's spread our wings and fly.

Let's begin this book with a prayer:

Dear God,

Please guide us on our journey, grant us the strength to transform our lives, and give us the courage to face and heal our fears and traumas. Help us to trust in our abilities and believe in the dreams we hold dear.

Thank you!

1
The Power of Daily Habit

Building a Powerful Daily Routine

Are you someone who often feels like you're running out of time, missing deadlines, or sacrificing what you want to do because you have no time? It's likely because you're drifting without a clear direction. By structuring your routine to align with your goals and purpose, you can become more energetic, productive, and even happier.

Most of us have been familiar with the term "routine" since childhood, and it continues to resonate throughout our lives. It holds particular significance for me because my father has a Navy background. Although the concept was always present during my childhood, I didn't fully realize its potential and advantages until I embraced it entirely in my own life.

A routine is more than just schedules or to-do lists; it's a set of activities you consistently perform to achieve specific outcomes. For example, making your bed is part of a routine, and the outcome is a sense of cleanliness and freshness. Establishing a powerful routine provides a sense of direction and clarity from the moment you wake up. Every deliberate action and mindful habit you cultivate weaves into the fabric of your future.

This way of living may initially sound like a life without freedom or flexibility. I thought so, too—until I discovered its remarkable benefits. Sticking to a routine is not about imposing restrictions; it's about creating structure, so you have time for everything.

Some people believe routines aren't for them, claiming they want to live a free, relaxed life without restrictions. However, a routine won't feel restrictive if it aligns with your needs and preferences. For instance, if you're a night owl, waking up early—say, at 4 a.m.—might not be ideal. In fact, it could feel disastrous, as your body typically enters deep sleep at that time. This doesn't mean you can't become an early riser; it simply requires gradual adjustments, like waking up 30 minutes earlier than usual and incrementally shifting to your desired time. If your routine isn't working for you, it's time to analyze it thoroughly and make adjustments.

How should one create a routine, and what factors should one consider while designing it? These are two major questions you may have. Before answering them, I will share a personal experience.

My parents are early birds, and seeing them wake up early made me want to wake up early, too. I tried it for many years, but I failed. The more I tried, the more I failed. I was unable to be consistent. My parents' body clocks are set for early mornings—they do not need an alarm to wake up. But I would easily sleep under the blanket if I didn't hear the morning loudness from my alarm. Sometimes, I even turned it off or snoozed it a hundred times to keep sleeping.

I continued hitting this loop for many years, building stress and frustration with the question inside me: *why them, not me?* The answer is simple: I didn't have a solid reason to wake up in the morning. To be precise, the things I used to do after I woke up early were not interesting or valuable enough to me, so I found them tedious. Identifying the purpose of every habit before you incorporate it into your routine is very important. Otherwise, you will hit the loop like I did.

After deep reflection and analysis, I realized that my parents being early birds is not a good enough reason for me to be one. I want to wake up early to get some quiet time in the morning when the world is still sleeping. I get to sit in a peaceful environment, look inside myself, and listen to my heart beating. Listening to my higher self and sitting in silence is something I love practicing in the morning. It gives me immense energy to perform all the challenging tasks and meet my personal and professional deadlines with high positivity and energy.

Now, I look forward every morning to waking up early so that I get to sit just with myself. See, I intentionally used *get* instead of any other phrase here. There is a difference between "I get to sit with myself" and "I sit with myself." The first shows that I am privileged to sit with myself, whereas the latter is neutral and straightforward. It doesn't carry any emotion or sense of being special. Think about it when you design your unique routine.

Here are some possible habits that you can consider when you design your routine:

- Making your bed
- Smiling at yourself in the mirror
- Exercising
- Journalling for clarity and growth
- Praying

- Practicing affirmations
- Practicing deep breathing
- Meditation or visualization
- Healing
- Scripting
- Practicing yoga
- Hydrating
- Eating a healthy breakfast
- Starting work at a consistent time
- Studying
- Reading a book
- Decluttering or tidying up your space
- Listening to podcasts
- Learning something new
- Going for a run or a walk
- Preparing for the next day
- Making a list of gratitude
- Reflecting on your day

Once you identify what you want to develop, arrange the tasks logically. For example, start by waking up early and making your bed, followed by hydrating yourself. Once the activities are organised in a logical sequence, assign a timeframe to each of them so you know what to expect next. For instance, when I wake up at 5 a.m., I know that by 5:20 a.m., I will be meditating, followed by visualization. This approach brings clarity, avoids chaos, and helps me mentally prepare for the next task. That's the benefit of a routine: you know what's coming and don't waste time deciding what to do next.

How Habits Evolve

A habit is an action you perform effortlessly and unconsciously—it comes naturally without requiring much thought, like taking a shower or brushing your teeth. However, introducing something new into your life as a habit requires regularity and consistency to become second nature. You can begin by incorporating the new habit into your routine. A routine is something you do consciously, with effort and intention. For example, if you want to develop a reading habit, you might start by reading just two pages each day. Initially, this will be part of your routine because you're deliberately making an effort. But over time, it will naturally transition into a habit.

Understanding this distinction is essential, as it forms the foundation for successfully adopting new habits and routines.

"You'll never change your life until you change something you do daily. The secret of your success is found in your daily routine."

John C. Maxwel

Activity: My Habits - Worksheet

Here is an activity designed to help you identify your current habits, including both positive and negative ones, and incorporate new meaningful habits into your routine. To begin, list your current daily habits in the table below. These could include actions like waking up at 9 a.m., scrolling through your phone, or making your bed.

No.	Current habits (both positive and negative)
1	
2	
3	
4	
5	
6	
7	
8	
9	
10	
11	
12	
13	
14	
15	

Now, identify the new habits you want to incorporate into your routine.

No.	New habits
1	
2	
3	
4	
5	
6	
7	
8	
9	
10	
11	
12	
13	
14	
15	

Now that you know the habits that you want to implement, start creating a personalised daily routine. For example, 5:00 a.m.—5:30 a.m., read a book.

From	To	Habit	Notes

Habit Formation and Tracking

Now that you have designed your to-be routine, let's look at how to implement the habits that will become part of your routine. Planning is always exciting and joyful, but implementing it takes time and effort. Most of us often get stuck in the planning phase by planning and re-planning. Taking small actions is the key.

Here are 10 principles that help in habit-forming and tracking.

Start small: Begin with easy, manageable habits

Human beings are ambitious and want to achieve everything at once. Starting small often seems insignificant when we focus on the overarching habits we aim to achieve. We want to see results quickly, so we think starting big will help us get there. However, we often stick to our routine for just a few days before reverting to our norm. Sometimes, we fall into a cycle of trying to implement everything at once, getting stuck, and starting over. After a few attempts, we conclude that it's either not for us or too hard to achieve. The issue isn't that you're incapable; it's the amount of load you're taking on.

Instead of trying to do everything at once, take small steps. If you want to start running 3 km, begin with a 30-minute brisk walk. Then, alternate between walking and light jogging until your body feels comfortable and ready for a 3 km run. This gradual approach prevents the change from feeling overwhelming. I'm not saying you can't attempt a 3 km run right away—you might have the willpower and dedication to start big. If you choose that path, be sure to monitor your progress. If you find yourself struggling, it might be a sign to slow down and take smaller steps. Everyone is different, so find what works best for you. Once you feel comfortable and confident with a 3 km run, move on to the next habit you want to adopt.

Be specific: Define your habits clearly

It is essential to clearly define the habits you want to incorporate for the successful implementation of a new routine. Imagine the satisfaction of having that habit seamlessly become second nature in your daily life. Then ask yourself: How will you make this happen? How do you plan to integrate the habit into your routine effectively?

To start, break the habit into multiple small tasks. Achieving these smaller tasks will not only help you incorporate the habit but also provide a sense of accomplishment and empowerment. For example, if you want to develop a reading habit, define aspects such as how many books you want to read, when you want that habit to become second nature, and how you plan to achieve it. A generic goal like "*I want to start reading*" lacks clarity, while a specific goal such as "*I want to read 12 self-help books by the end of 2025*" provides clear direction.

You can break this goal down further: "*I want to read at least one self-help book every month.*" This approach allows you to track progress and brings greater clarity. Clear, specific goals make it easier for your brain to form the habit compared to vague ones.

When you break down a new habit into smaller chunks of tasks, ensure to incorporate the following elements:

- Frequency: How many times would you like to perform this? Once a day, once a week, or once a month?
- Time: When do you plan to perform the task? Is it right before bedtime, during morning tea, or before bed?
- Place: Is there a particular location in your house where you want to perform this task?
- Duration: How long would you require to complete this task?
- An action you want to perform: What action are you thinking of taking? For instance, it can be taking short breaks to hydrate yourself, going for an evening walk, or even practicing stillness for 1 minute.

Stack habits: Link new habits to existing ones

Habit stacking is a fantastic technique to build new habits by linking the new habit with an existing one. For example, we brush our teeth every day without needing reminders. It has become second nature to brush as soon as we get up and enter the washroom. Stack a new habit you're trying to form along with this. Suppose you want to practice affirmations; this could be a good pair, as you'd be standing in front of the mirror. You can practice affirmations right after finishing brushing. In brief, you incorporate your new desired habit right after an established one. This way, you will be able to perform the desired habit regularly.

Here are some habit-stacking combinations that worked well for me.

- Drink a glass of water as soon as you wake up.
- Meditate while your morning tea or coffee is brewing.
- Practice journaling while enjoying your morning tea or coffee.
- Plan for the next day before you finish your work.
- Go for a walk in your garden once you finish your work.
- Floss once you have dinner.
- Read a book before bedtime.

Be consistent: Aim for daily practice

I can't emphasize the importance of consistency enough. Showing up for yourself is essential to building a new habit into your routine. It creates momentum, helping you stick to the plan for the long term. Each small yet consistent action reinforces the habit, eventually making it a natural part of your routine. By being consistent, regardless of how much you achieve, you are contributing to forming a solid habit.

Suppose you are trying to incorporate exercise into your routine. As a beginner, you may want to start small. If your goal is to perform 20 minutes of exercise daily, ensure you show up consistently. Even if you manage only 10 minutes on a particular day, showing up remains crucial. This approach strengthens the neural pathways in your brain. By maintaining consistency for some time—say, a couple of months—you increase the likelihood of continuing the habit as your brain adapts accordingly.

When I first started exercising, it felt energizing and uplifting. I was full of enthusiasm and thrilled by the new habit. I even relished the post-workout soreness, convinced it was a sign the exercises were already working on my body fat. However, over three weeks, my enthusiasm began to wane. Workouts became less intriguing, more time-consuming, and increasingly tedious.

When I wasn't in the mood to hit the gym, I didn't pressure myself by forcing it; instead, I worked out at home. Every day is different, and you can't expect to do everything perfectly. By choosing to exercise at home, I stayed consistent with my habits and felt happier because I didn't give up for a lame reason. We are intelligent and resourceful enough to tackle problems and find alternative solutions as long as we remain determined. Remember, the simple act of showing up can be the most motivating thing you do for yourself.

Track progress: Use a simple tracker

One of the tasks I enjoy in habit formation is tracking progress. It gives me immense pleasure to strike off a completed task as part of the process. I don't know how many of you can relate, but it's another source of inspiration for me. Tracking your progress helps build a sense of accountability. It motivates you by showing how far you've come. When I look at my habit tracker, I see it's just two more days to complete a month of habit-building. Knowing this and seeing the progress on paper motivates me to stick to the routine, even during a busy schedule.

You can use any type of tracker to monitor your progress and consistency—the options are endless. I use an A4 paper tracker template because I prefer the tactile experience over typing online.

Here is a habit tracker template to help you stay accountable and visualize your progress.

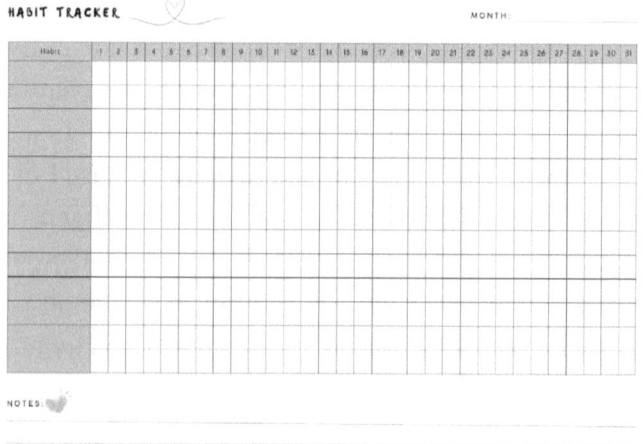

Ready to take the first step towards effective habit tracking? You can scan the QR code below to download the tracker template for free. It's time to start your journey towards accountability and visualize your progress.

Use reminders: Set alarms or leave notes

When starting a new habit, it is possible to forget about it. This act may not be intentional. I have encountered similar situations when practicing the 369 manifestation technique. I had to write a positive statement three times a day: 3 times in the morning, 6 times in the afternoon, and 9 times in the evening. This method is known as the 369 manifestation. It was easy to forget to write it during the 33-day period. Hence, I set up a reminder on my phone to ensure I remembered to write it. I also placed sticky notes on my fridge and mirror—places I frequently visited. This way, I remained consistent while completing the manifestation technique. Sometimes, our minds overlook tasks, especially if they're unfamiliar to us. Reminders and sticky notes are great ways to keep ourselves on track.

Be patient: Habits take time to form

Hold your horses! It's normal for us to demand instant gratification. Habits take time to form. While some habits are easier to develop, others may require more time. If we attempt to expedite the process by sacrificing the calibre of our input, it will only last for a while. Additionally, it could lead to burnout. Remember the long-term goal and maintain your consistency.

Celebrate small wins: Acknowledge your progress

Celebrations are an excellent way to elevate your energy and motivation. When you hit a milestone in your goal, such as completing two weeks of journalling, celebrate it. A celebration can take any form, from cutting a cake to enjoying a spa day. It depends on your needs and circumstances. But it's an opportunity to pat yourself on the back and say, "Well done, this is great." Sometimes, these small acts of celebration give us the motivation boost needed to move from where we are to where we want to be.

Here are some ideas to celebrate your small wins:

- Self-care, such as a spa day at home, a massage, or even spending time in nature
- Have your favourite food
- Buy yourself flowers
- Give yourself a day off from your chores if your schedule permits
- Buy yourself something that you've been wanting for a long time
- Go for any activities that excite you, like kayaking or camping
- Do art journaling about your success
- Go for a picnic with friends
- Go on a shopping spree
- Host a movie night at your house
- Perform a karaoke
- Take a mid-day nap that you've been missing out

Tip: Plan the celebration before reaching the milestone; otherwise, you might spend more time thinking about how to celebrate than actually celebrating.

Learn from failure: Use failures as learning opportunities

Failures are often depicted in a negative light, but I see them as valuable learning opportunities. Without failure, how can you truly appreciate the meaning of success? However, never let failure make you give up on something. You might be tired of hearing this, but it's a powerful statement.

There could be setbacks—we might miss a swim lesson, skip a podcast, or take a break from exercise. That's okay; it's not the end of the world. Rise up and start again from where you left off. Missing a day or two of a habit, or even taking a break, is not a big deal as long as it's done consciously. Our minds might need a pause, and our bodies need rest. But once you feel energetic again, return to the habit you've been practicing.

If you're taking a longer break than you think is appropriate, it's a good idea to reflect on it. Consider what you could do differently to make it more engaging. Suppose you're tired of cooking healthy food—think of other possibilities. You could order homemade food, buy pre-chopped vegetables to save prep time, grow a vegetable garden and cook from your harvest for added joy, share the responsibility with your partner, or cook together while playing music to make the experience more enjoyable. There are many options available if you look closely. Identify a viable solution and continue on your journey.

Failures are steps to success. Learn from them, reflect, and move forward.

Review regularly: Assess your habits regularly

Review and reflect continuously to monitor your progress and determine if any adjustments are needed to your plan and approach. Regular reflection helps you stay on track and reach your final destination. How often should you review and reflect? The answer is—it's up to you. Personally, I like to reflect on my exercise progress every four weeks. First, because I'm curious to see how much I've progressed during that time; second, it helps me identify where to focus next and what changes to implement. Based on this, I update my workout plan.

However, for salsa dance practice, I review my progress quarterly since I only attend one lesson per week. You can decide how frequently to reflect and adjust based on the regularity and impact of your activity. When reflecting, focus on what's working well, what isn't, and what improvements you'd like to make in relation to the duration of your goal or habit. As we learn and grow, these reflections are essential for aligning with the habits we're cultivating.

For example, if you've been journaling in the same format or book for a year, it might be time to revisit your approach and make it more engaging. Small changes like these can significantly impact your motivation and strengthen your mindset.

Effective Planning and Task Management

Creating to-do lists and trackers can be rewarding if used appropriately. If you have a packed schedule and are trying to incorporate a new habit into your routine, trackers and to-do lists can serve as invaluable tools to help you stay organised and make intentional progress. Here are some perspectives on using to-do lists and planners.

Creating daily to-do lists

If you enjoy visualizing and having a tactile experience, I recommend using paper trackers and to-do lists. I use them all the time, and the benefits are truly excellent. I understand that printing them out and writing with a pen or pencil can be time-consuming, but I promise the results are worth it.

I also carry a book dedicated solely to my to-do list. It might be considered old-fashioned, but writing down my vague or random thoughts and tasks in this book gives me clarity and peace of mind. Carrying too many thoughts in your head can often feel chaotic and overwhelming. However, the simple act of jotting them down in a notebook or on paper brings immediate relief and clarity. Once you write them down, they're out of your mind. You can then see the tasks that were troubling you laid out on paper, almost as if you're visualizing them. This method is highly effective.

Another aspect of writing a to-do list is that you can review it quickly, prioritise tasks, and plan your days accordingly.

When I'm swamped with tasks, I create multiple to-do lists: one for shifting home, one for work-related tasks, and another for home management, such as paying bills or mowing the lawn. This practice helps me organise my to-dos across different areas of life, like work and home, allowing me to focus on one thing at a time. It brings clarity to my mind and a sense of lightness, making tasks feel more manageable and less overwhelming. If you prefer digital tools, there are numerous apps available for creating notes and to-do lists. The key is to find a method that suits your lifestyle and preferences.

Weekly and monthly planning strategies

Weekly and monthly planners help you prioritise your days and goals. Before the start of each month, I prepare a monthly planner with sections for the key focus of the month, to-do lists, important dates, and notes. This way, when planning the upcoming month, I know what to expect and how to mentally prepare. For example, if one of my critical tasks as part of habit development is decluttering my house, I write it under the key focus section. Since it might take one or two days of my weekend, I plan it in advance and discuss it with my partner. This helps me mentally prepare for the task and approach it with a clear mindset, ensuring I accomplish it efficiently. I firmly believe that being mentally prepared is half the battle. Monthly trackers can also be used for critical to-dos or goals tied to habits. Striking out or ticking off a completed task instantly brings immense pleasure, a sense of achievement, and satisfaction.

Boost your productivity with these free, downloadable planning tools.

Whether you prefer daily, weekly, or monthly planning, these templates will help you organize your tasks, prioritize effectively, and achieve your goals.

Final Thoughts

- When you introduce a new habit into your lifestyle, make sure to stay flexible. For instance, if you practice manifestation every morning but cannot due to an unexpected change, be flexible and try practicing it in the afternoon or evening instead. This is better than not practicing at all. Remember, consistency matters.
- Gradually integrate new habits into your life instead of implementing multiple habits altogether.
- Never Give Up: Remember, persistence is the key to success.
- Establish a consistent sleep schedule to adjust your circadian rhythm. Thus, falling asleep and waking up at the preferred times will become natural to you.

- Prepare the night before for a smooth morning. This will give you the energy to start your day early with a clear purpose. Utilise trackers, to-do lists, and apps that support this.

- Be open to creating an environment that supports your goals and aspirations. Your mind is your house; keep it clean. If you fill it with junk, it will reflect in your thoughts and actions.

- Recognise that there will always be a dip in motivation at certain points along the way. This is quite normal. Bringing self-awareness and making appropriate adjustments is what you need to do. If you feel you're hitting the wall, do not hesitate to seek assistance from friends or family. Sometimes, we underestimate our circle and assume they may not know the answer. They may have addressed the issue and already overcome the obstacle ahead of us.

- Consider having accountability partners. Having someone with whom you can share your progress and challenges can be motivating. Whether it's a friend, family member, or someone with similar goals, an accountability partner can help you stay on track and provide the encouragement you need.

Key Points to Remember

- A routine is a set of actions performed regularly that provides structure, direction, and purpose, helping to create clarity and consistency in daily life.
- A routine does not limit one's freedom; it creates a framework that helps you prioritise and stay focused on your goals and dreams.
- Design a routine that supports and aligns with your needs. Everyone is different, and what works for me may not necessarily work for you.
- Break down habits you want to develop into smaller chunks of tasks; use trackers to celebrate your progress.
- It is important to maintain consistency if you want to incorporate a habit into your routine. Start with an easy habit and gradually build on it.
- Treat failures as learning curves; regularly reflect on what's working well and not, and make necessary adjustments as you go.

2
The Ultimate Self-Upgrade

Discovering Your Core Values

Values are the pillars that influence our decisions, behaviour, and characteristics. We consciously or subconsciously draw upon our values numerous times throughout the day, whether navigating a major decision, reconciling with a friend or family member, or choosing the right action for the moment. If gratitude is one of your values, you're the kind of person who consistently sees the positive in any situation and expresses thanks for the good. You find greatness in simple things, appreciate them deeply, and derive happiness and peace from this mindset. It's natural for you to focus on the good rather than the bad.

Identifying your values is necessary because you can use them to make crucial decisions, draw a boundary (to set priority), and receive a sense of direction in your life. For me, inner peace is essential. Whenever I have a silly argument or a dispute with my dear ones, my values play a significant role in guiding me. They prompt me to reflect on what I stand to gain from the argument and whether it's worth the effort. These thoughts help me regain my sense of peace and approach the situation with a calmer, more constructive energy. On the other hand, if I were to continue arguing, I know I'd end up losing my inner peace and regretting the entire conversation. Values hold a central place in my life, often influencing my decisions and actions in ways so natural that I sometimes overlook their importance.

Another value of mine was mental and physical health. I used 'was' intentionally and will explain why in the next paragraph. For me, physical and mental health holistically means regular exercise, healthy eating, drinking water, work-life balance, sleeping 7 hours, mindfulness and meditation, etc. These elements are now instilled in me, so they come naturally to my life without any effort or reminders.

Once you identify your values and integrate them into your life, they become a guiding framework for your decisions and actions. However, it's important to acknowledge that values can evolve over time as you encounter new experiences. As you grow, values outgrow, too. The values you hold today may not feel as significant to you in two years. This shift could result from personal growth, changing circumstances, or new experiences. Reflecting on and reassessing your values over time is a worthwhile practice. My value of 'mental and physical health' has evolved over time and shifted toward spiritual growth. With a solid mental and physical well-being foundation, my priorities have expanded to explore broader aspects of life. Today, I focus more on my inner self—engaging in meditation, healing, and delving into spiritual teachings and practices.

Now that we have discussed values and their importance, let's explore how to identify values closer to you. The following are some of the questions that will help you identify your values. Ensure you sit in a peaceful environment without any external disturbance. Take a couple of breaths in and out to calm yourself down. Then, ask yourself the following questions. Feel free to use a pen and paper.

- What is most important to you?

- What do you prioritise the most?
- What makes you happy?
- What makes you call a day good?
- What energises you?
- What drains you?
- What is it that you cannot live with?
- What is it that you cannot compromise?
- When did you feel the most proud and happy? What values were present then?
- What is your vision for the next 2-3 years?
- What supports you in achieving your vision, and what doesn't?
- What are the core areas of your life that are important to you, such as health, career, family, inner peace, etc.?

Once you answer the above questions, you will identify a pattern of what is most important to you and what drains you.

Activity: Values Clarification Exercise

In this section, we will explore some common values to help you identify which ones resonate most closely with you. Start by choosing 10 values from the list, then narrow it down to the 3-5 that resonate most with you. Embed these values in your mind so that every action you take is in alignment with them. I write down my values on paper and stick them to my corkboard so that my day starts by looking at them and reaffirming what matters most to me. Remember to reassess your values over time!

List of values

Forgiveness	Creativity	Wisdom
Empathy	Dignity	Kindness
Accountability	Humility	Curiosity
Gratitude	Family	Courage
Mental Health	Spirituality	Leadership
Physical Health	Honesty	Loyalty
Determination	Punctuality	Exploration
Sincerity	Achievement	Resilience
Bravery	Competence	Respect
Equality	Friendship	Self-esteem
Authenticity	Adventurous	Passion
Progression	Trust	Power
Fun	Peace	Appreciation
Harmony	Success	Self-care
Generosity	Integrity	Flexibility
Dedication	Sustainability	Optimism
Joy	Open-mindedness	Awareness
Learning	Service	Active
Wealth	Collaboration	Excellence

Creating A Vision Board

A vision board visually represents your goals, dreams, and aspirations. An ideal vision board may have a representation of goals from all eight areas of your life, such as

- Health
- Relationship
- Family
- Inner Peace
- Fun
- Finance & wealth
- Professional development and
- Personal development

Having a vision board offers many benefits. It inspires and motivates you to take action and achieve your goals within a specific timeframe. A vision board helps you understand and visualize your goals more clearly by keeping your focus on specific objectives rather than dividing your attention across multiple unrelated goals. By looking at your vision board daily, you signal to your subconscious that this is where you want to land. You reinforce the important goals you want to prioritise and achieve within a set timeframe. It provides clarity and a sense of purpose, helping you stay grounded rather than drifting aimlessly.

Visual representation feeds into your mind and manifests faster. When I immersed myself in my vision board, I noticed that I started taking action towards some of my goals without even realising it. Visualizing your dreams through images and sketches on a vision board becomes more tangible, especially because you've put time and effort into creating them. I believe that at that point, the process is already halfway done because you've imprinted the image of your goal on your mind. This is one of the reasons you begin taking action, often without even realising it—your mind is already aligned with the vision, and it starts guiding you toward the right steps. Your mind automatically identifies the right opportunities that align with your goals. It's a powerful method for visualizing and achieving your goals more quickly. While it doesn't mean you can skip taking action—because action is necessary for every goal—the process becomes easier once you start visualizing and manifesting your desires. It feels as though the universe begins aligning everything needed to make your goals and dreams come true. All you have to do is recognise those opportunities and seize them.

You can create a vision board on a foam, a cork board or a digital one. Choosing the style that suits you the most is up to you. You can use images, quotes, affirmations, or drawings from the internet or magazines to create a vision board. I rely on the Pinterest app to download images and quotes. Once you have collected the images online, you can print them and arrange them on a board. It is a fun activity to arrange and re-arrange them until you are delighted with the final look of your vision board. A tip is to use images of different sizes, colours, and fonts to bring a vibrant feel to your vision board. Again, it is up to you how you want to create it. Once you stick them to the board, you can find a perfect place to hang it. I suggest hanging it at a place where you visit often or spend most of your time during the day. This way, you can create a lasting impression on your subconscious mind. If you are creating a digital version, Canva is a good starting point for creating your vision board. You can use your vision board as wallpaper or screensaver on your laptop and mobile phone.

A concrete vision board is most effective when your goals are specific. I prefer setting specific goals, which is why my vision boards are more detailed rather than generic, like simply writing *'Dancing'*. For example, if I want to learn Salsa, I gather images of that specific dance style or include text that specifically says *'Salsa'* on my board. This level of specificity helps focus my intentions and makes the vision more real.

You can create your vision board for one, three, or five years—it doesn't matter. I prefer one year, as I enjoy the process and like breaking down big, complex goals into smaller ones to see the results. You can revisit your vision board occasionally to check if it needs updates, especially if you've had it for over a year. As your goals and desires evolve, it's a good idea to update your vision board by replacing outdated images or adding new ones. A vision board isn't something you create once and leave unchanged. You can use it flexibly, adapting it however you like.

It's also important to reflect on your progress and celebrate your successes, no matter how big or small. Celebrating sends a signal to your brain, triggering the release of dopamine, which brings happiness and motivation. It also helps reinforce your aspirations. And who doesn't love a celebration?

Here are some illustrations of different vision boards I created in the past years for reference.

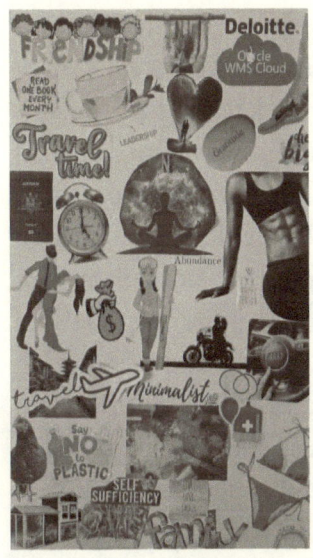 

Creating a Bucket List

A bucket list is essentially a list of all your dreams throughout your lifetime. Anything you may want to experience or achieve can find a place on your bucket list. It ranges from personal goals like learning yoga or mastering a new language to adventurous activities like bungee jumping or skydiving. There are no set limitations to it. Imagine living without any restrictions or limitations—how would you live your life? Picture it on your bucket list. It could be something simple, like spending a weekend at the beach or going to a spa, or more complex, like exploring Europe or moving to the countryside to enjoy a slower pace of life. It all depends on your wishes and goals. The fun part of creating a bucket list is using your imagination to design your life without limitations.

You can create a bucket list in digital or physical form. I have a book dedicated to this, where I draw, write down, or paste pictures related to each bucket list item. This approach amplifies my dreams and gives them wings. If you feel stuck or unsure where to begin, take a moment to imagine how you would feel after achieving a goal or dream. Use those emotions to inspire and strengthen your bucket list, making your dreams feel more tangible and achievable. Writing down your dreams and visualizing them as already accomplished creates a blueprint for them to manifest in real life. Since they have already materialized in your mind, what happens in reality is simply the first manifestation of your vision coming to life. This connection aligns your efforts with your dreams, making the process feel natural and inevitable. By putting your goal on paper, you take the first step toward making it a reality. Dreams are said to manifest more easily when brought into focus.

Here are some pages from my bucket list for reference.

Once you identify your goals and dreams, make a list of them. Again, you can apply the eight areas discussed in the previous section to ensure you have balanced dreams and goals. You can also create it for shorter periods, like one for Autumn and another for Spring. It is up to you how you want to design your bucket list.

Here are some sample bucket list items if you like to take some inspiration.

- Swim with sharks
- Kite surf
- Abseil down a cliff
- Experience camping
- Flip on a trampoline
- Adopt a child
- Swim with tortoise
- Six-pack abs
- Say No to restaurant food
- Live sustainably
- Build a veggie garden
- Build a cottage garden
- Raise chickens in the backyard
- Have butterflies in the garden
- Whale watching
- Take parents on a trip
- Travel on a business class
- Star gazing
- Build an outdoor brick oven
- Parasail
- Donate blood
- Try ziplining
- Kiss a stranger
- Milk a cow
- Fly a kite
- Adopt a dog
- Ride jetski
- Eat healthy
- Say no to plastics
- Own a house
- Play Holi
- Wear a bikini
- Hug a tree
- Mentor students
- Record a song
- Try hookah
- Trip with besties
- Get a tattoo
- Kiss in the rain
- Snowboard

Experience snow	Go canoeing
Explore Finland during Christmas	Bake a cake
Ride in a luge	Try hot pools
Unplug for a weekend	Wine tasting
Camp in the backyard	Teach a subject
Build a flower bed	Make a soap
Get a college degree	Experience farm life
Horseback ride on the beach	Start a blog
Get engaged or married	Dance on a bar
Send a message in a bottle	Drink at an ice bar
Go on a blind date	Volunteer
Witness the aurora borealis	Create a family tree
Learn a new language	Buy a campervan
Watch sunrise or sunset	Attend a foam party
Stay in a five start hotel	Take a mud bath
Read 20 books a year	Donate organs
Wear a wig for the day	Do a cleanse
Create a photo book for every year	Start a business
Celebrate white Christmas	Plant a tree
Be a self-made millionaire	Write a book

Create a passive income	Win a lottery
Save 3 months of expenses	Climb a tree
Sleep on a satin sheet	Start B&B
Be in the newspaper or magazine	Stay up all night
Dye a crazy hair color	Smell roses
Invest in mutual funds	Build a routine
Wear a Halloween costume	Write an e-book
Learn to use chopsticks	Go for a bike trip
Make yoghurt at home	Learn meditation
Start a youtube channel	Fall in love (again)
Live abroad	Get your dream job
Knit a sweater	Host a party
Go on a cruise	Get married
Take a first aid course	Walk on a glacier
Ride an ATV	Run a workshop
Take a driver's license	Retire early
Try Reiki	Go vegetarian

Once you create a bucket list, it is essential to prioritize the items based on the level of excitement, time constraints, and importance. If you have complex bucket list items, you can break them into smaller ones. One of the items on my bucket list was to explore Western Australia. I broke it down into smaller chunks by writing down the major towns I want to explore in Western Australia. This will give me clarity while making small wins towards my big dream. I'd also suggest adding 1-3 bucket list items that excite you for the year to your vision board. When doing so, be sure to consider the dependencies, such as money, time, skills, etc. Based on the complexities, planning would be required for some of the bucket list items.

Once you complete a dream goal or wish from your bucket list, mark it as "Done." This lets you see all the accomplishments you've made and the dreams you've conquered in one place. It can also boost your energy and inspiration to achieve more. You could even add photos or memories from the experience to your bucket list if you like. The more creative you make it, the more fun and engaging it will be!

The 101 Life Goals

If you don't consider yourself a creative person or don't have much time to dedicate to a bucket list, you can simply create a list of 101 life goals and dreams. Take a sheet of paper or a notebook and write your goals in the SMART format. This approach helps you track your goals daily and tick them off as you complete them.

You can include both short-term and long-term goals in various areas. For example, reading one book this month could be a short-term goal, while saving for your dream house over the next five years might be a long-term goal. Adding goals with varying levels of effort—such as simple, easily achievable, moderate, and complex—is also a great idea. This way, you'll see some goals already ticked off, giving you a sense of achievement and motivation to keep going.

SMART goals are a popular framework to set realistic goals that can be achieved in a specific period. SMART stands for Specific, Measurable, Achievable, Relevant, and Time-bound. It essentially says your goal needs to be:

- Specific: Ask yourself what exactly you are trying to achieve.
- Measurable: How do you intend to track the progress of your goal?
- Achievable: Is your goal achievable, given your circumstances?
- Relevant: Ask yourself if your goal aligns with your values and long-term vision.
- Time-bound: When do you intend to achieve the goal in terms of a deadline?

Here are some examples of smart goals in some areas of life.

- I want to read 12 self-help books in the next 12 months.
- I want to lose 4 kg by *Month 20XX*.
- I want to learn C++ programming by the end of next month.
- I want to enrol in swimming lessons tomorrow.
- I want to save $10,000 by *Month 20XX*.

- I want to start a small veggie garden in my backyard in the next six months.
- I want to visit five countries within five years and learn about different cultures.
- I want to become a project manager within the next five years and gain relevant experience.

Once you create SMART goals, you can apply a micro-goal strategy to break them down into monthly, weekly, or daily targets. This approach allows you to achieve your goals more easily while also tracking your progress.

For example, consider the goal: "*I want to save $10,000 by December 2025.*" To save $10,000 in a year, you can break it into smaller goals, such as saving $850 each month for the next 12 months. Then, evaluate whether this amount is achievable and realistic. If saving that much isn't feasible, consider alternative ways to meet the goal—such as taking on an additional part-time job, reducing expenses, cooking at home, and limiting eating out. In short, make your goals smaller, achievable, and realistic. Then, you can log these into monthly trackers to ensure the goal remains part of your focus for the month. By doing this, you take consistent steps toward achieving larger goals.

"Setting goals is the first step in turning the invisible into the visible."

Tony Robbins

Embracing a Positive Mindset

An open and positive mindset is not just important; it's transformative. It is the key to growth, welcoming change, and embracing new opportunities. What you think becomes your reality. If you feed your mind with positivity, you become more of a positive thinker, and vice versa.

It is said that we have approximately 80,000 thoughts per day, meaning we process thousands of thoughts every hour. But have you ever wondered what kind of thoughts pass through your mind most often? For an ordinary person, many of these are likely to be self-doubt, worries, frustrations, hesitations, anxiety, and other negative thoughts. However, with the power of positive thinking, these can be transformed into opportunities for growth and change. The benefits of this shift are immense: increased resilience, improved relationships, and a more fulfilling life.

So, how can we stay positive? To stay positive, you can begin by monitoring your thoughts. Practice consciousness and self-awareness. If you observe your thoughts without reacting and simply let them pass, they will eventually fade away. Watch them as a third person without reacting. This is one way to achieve a state of thoughtlessness.

Once you start monitoring your thoughts, you will begin to understand their patterns—whether they are positive, sceptical, motivational, or negative. If you become aware that a thought is negative, you can monitor it and become self-aware. This is the first step in overcoming negative thoughts. Once you identify a negative thought, transform it into a positive statement. For instance, if you are stuck in traffic and feel frustrated or stressed, realising you might be late to work, avoid blaming or dwelling on negativity. Instead, focus on positive actions, such as listening to music or a podcast, informing a colleague that you will be a few minutes late to reduce tension, or reflecting on how you can leave earlier the next day to avoid the situation. By practicing this shift in mindset, you can avoid unnecessary frustration and negative energy, fostering personal growth and inner peace. These small actions make a significant difference in building a peaceful life.

Once you start transforming doubtful, negative thoughts into positive ones, you begin to change. You start finding happiness in everything, appreciating more and staying grateful for what you have. Life becomes more beautiful and magical. However, this doesn't happen out of the blue. Continuous practice and effort are required to build a positive mindset. Practicing gratitude is a fantastic way to stay positive. It helps you appreciate the people and things in your life rather than assigning blame. Gratitude is also a powerful tool that shifts your focus from what's lacking to what's abundant. To practice gratitude, you can start with a journal. If you're a beginner, consider using a gratitude journal with prompts. Otherwise, a simple diary or freestyle journal works just as well. You can also begin expressing gratitude to the people or things around you as situations arise. For instance, you might express gratitude to your house, trees, bees, friends, family, neighbours, wealth, health, books, or even a pen—anything whose presence enriches your life. The more you practice gratitude, the more happiness and positivity will flow into your life.

Reflecting on your thoughts and emotions is also a good idea to stay positive. Analyse how you handled any problematic situations or challenges in your day. Was it positive or negative? If it wasn't positive, what was it, and how did you handle it? Self-reflection is a powerful tool that can help you identify and address negative thought patterns. It is also helpful to reflect on how you can shift more toward the positive side next time. Sometimes, we over-criticise ourselves for simple things, but reflection can help us overcome this. Engaging in self-reflection allows us to cultivate compassion and become more considerate toward ourselves. Lastly, monitor your language—pay attention to the words you use in conversations and self-talk. What we say reveals a great deal about our mindset.

Embracing growth and learning

Being open to learning and exploring new ideas and experiences can also contribute to a positive mindset. We learn from life's experiences and challenges, but the key question is: how do you perceive these challenges? Are they your enemies or friends? Consider them as an opportunity to grow, learn, and build confidence. It doesn't mean you must continuously challenge yourself or choose challenging opportunities. However, having an appetite to push yourself from your comfort zone and welcome good challenges is better than fearing failure. This way, you learn something, telling your brain that you can face challenging situations. Once you overcome challenging situations that push you out of your comfort zone, the happiness, satisfaction, and confidence gained from maintaining an open mindset become essential for personal growth.

Next, let's move on to failures. How do you perceive failures? What emotions come to mind when you think of the word 'failure?' Is it disappointment, embarrassment, frustration, relief, or reflection? Failure triggers different emotions for different people. For me, it is a reflection that something didn't work, and I may need to stay open and learn from it. It feels more like another opportunity to improve, achieve better outcomes, and continue learning.

There is nothing wrong if failure triggers a negative emotion in you. You can change it by redefining failure as feedback. Reflect on a failure and see what it is trying to teach you and what you can learn from it. Then, when you try again, focus on the process and steps rather than the results. This itself would make a huge difference. Our mind plays a huge role in how we see and perceive things. Start to see failure as a new experience or a motivation to grow even better. This shift in perspective empowers you to take control of your growth and development. Looking at things with curiosity is another way to embrace growth. Rather than having fear or anxiety, look at the possibilities with curiosity. Curiosity naturally pushes you to explore various experiences, ask questions, and view things from different perspectives, which helps you continuously improve.

Practicing acceptance

Now, let's explore the practice of acceptance and surrender. Do you worry a lot about the future or the things that are not under your control? If so, this section is for you. I have been there, and I know the anxiety and burst of emotions it creates when you can't help yourself by taking control or making a decision. Sometimes, life asks you to let go of certain things to create space for new opportunities and experiences to enter your life. '*Let go*' is such a powerful phrase that could work magic for you. If you have emotions that are not helping you stay positive and move forward in life, just let them go! But how can one let go? I will tell you. If you are feeling anxious about your exam results, which are due next week, first acknowledge the emotions and be aware of them. Say to yourself, "I am feeling anxious now, and it's okay." Do not judge the emotion—just acknowledge it. Say to your anxiety, "I see you, and I feel you." Full stop. This act of acknowledgement can bring a profound sense of freedom and liberation, allowing you to focus on what you can control and empowering you to move forward.

Once you acknowledge the unwanted emotion that you're experiencing, make a list of actions you can take to address it. In the above example, you can best distract yourself from negative emotions by engaging in an exciting activity, such as committing to volunteer work or creating a scrapbook. This way, you can shift your focus from anxiety to something that you can control, empowering you and reducing the feeling of being overwhelmed. If this doesn't work for you, ask '*then what*' questions to yourself. Suppose you have anxiety because, in one of the subjects, you may not get an A+. So ask '*then what?*' You may not get admission to the college you wanted to join as first preference. Then what? Then, you may have to enter the second college that you shortlisted. Then what? Then you join there, and life continues with new challenges. It is not the end of the world, even though we may feel so initially. Life will continue as it is destined to unfold. Practicing this approach helps you confront and navigate the worst-case scenario with a clearer mind and a lighter heart. Letting go of fears and worries opens the door to possibilities and opportunities beyond your imagination and expectations. So just let go!

Lastly, I'd like to introduce a powerful method called surrender. Surrender is the process of withdrawing from everything and surrendering all your fear and emotional baggage to the supreme power. If you believe in God, surrender everything to God; if you believe in the universe or a divine power, then surrender to them. By surrendering, you transfer all your negative emotions, weaknesses, and hesitations to that powerful entity, allowing you to return to a peaceful state of mind.

You can surrender your worries and doubts to the supreme power in many ways—through prayer, meditation, or even by writing a letter. If you choose prayer, you might affirm, "I surrender all my worries to you; please guide and heal me through you." Then, let it go—the universe will take care of the rest. If you prefer meditation, start by taking a few deep breaths. Visualize transferring all your worries and anxiety into a shining white divine bowl. Imagine a little fairy approaching, taking the bowl, and flying away with it, symbolising that your worries are being taken away and cared for by the angels. By the end of this meditation, you should feel light and relieved.

Alternatively, you can surrender through writing a letter to the divine power. Write down all your worries, fully surrendering them to the power you believe in. Continue writing until you feel you've completely let everything out. Once finished, you can burn the paper, imagining your worries vanishing and being taken care of by the divine power. For some, writing brings clarity and helps release everything from their minds onto the page. If this resonates with you, writing may be the best option.

Prompts for Positive Mindset

The following reflection questions are designed to help you foster a growth mindset and maintain a positive outlook. These prompts will encourage you to reframe challenges and view them as opportunities for growth while staying grateful. If you practice journaling, you can use the following prompts to guide your reflections and help foster a positive mindset.

- Affirmations for today
- Five things that you're grateful for
- What went well today?
- What didn't go well and why?
- Do you want to make any improvements or take corrective action to avoid such situations?
- Describe a personal strength you used today. How did it help you?
- Describe a challenge you faced recently. What did you learn from it?

- What's one small step you can take tomorrow towards a big goal?
- What's a recent "failure" you can reframe as a learning opportunity?
- Any limiting belief you hold, and how do you reframe it positively?

Remember, a positive mindset is something you can cultivate over time; it's not something you develop all of a sudden. Along the journey, you learn, relearn, make mistakes, and learn from them. You reflect, continuously surrender, and ground yourself. As you progress, the path becomes clearer, and the light will gradually reveal itself to you.

Key Points to Remember

- There are various methods and tools, such as vision boards, 101 life goals, and bucket lists, that can help you set goals and dreams. Without dreams, life is like a boat drifting aimlessly. Spread your wings and fly!
- Values form the foundation that shapes our decisions, actions, and personal traits. Identifying your values is crucial for your growth and living a peaceful, fulfilling life.
- A positive mindset is something you develop along the journey. It's essential to be aware of your thoughts and the nature of those thoughts. Practice shifting negative thoughts to positive ones by focusing on the brighter side and considering how you can avoid similar situations in the future.
- Let go of resistance and allow things to flow to you—things beyond your imagination and expectations.
- Embrace failure, as it's an opportunity for reflection and growth. Failure helps you become a better version of yourself and learn to handle challenges more effectively.

3

Pathways to Mental Wellness

Meditation

When I was first told to practice meditation, I immediately thought that it was only for saints and spiritual lightworkers – people far removed from the hustle and bustle of everyday life. I was so unaware of the concept of meditation, especially considering my mom had been practicing it since her early days. But deep down, I knew I would eventually embrace it, as I strongly believed I had many of my mom's wonderful traits (which I'm incredibly proud of). Years passed, and my sister joined my mom on her spiritual journey, but I observed all of this without feeling any turbulence. I thought meditation just wasn't for me. Then, a storm passed through my life, changing my course and prompting me to look at life through a different lens. That was the turning point when I began to explore meditation and visualization. Once I started practicing, I began to experience its benefits. It helped me stay calm and focused while providing mental clarity and inner peace.

Meditation offers numerous benefits; it fosters mindfulness – being fully present in the moment and aware of your thoughts, emotions, body, and surroundings. This mindfulness helps you remain focused on the present, free from distractions. I used to daydream frequently during work meetings, and when I returned to the conversation, I often struggled to reconnect with what was being discussed. This improved dramatically after I began practicing meditation. I became more aware of distractions and could easily bring myself back to the present moment. I'm not saying distractions won't happen, but you'll become more conscious of them and better able to regain focus quickly. The mindfulness developed through meditation enables you to respond to situations in a healthier, more positive way rather than reacting impulsively. By quieting your mind, you'll think more clearly and make better decisions.

How should one practice meditation? Meditation is listening to your breaths and reaching a no-thought state. To reach that no-thought state, start by observing the thoughts that pass through your mind as a third person without any restriction. This allows you to detach from your thoughts, reducing their power over your feelings and emotions. When you view your thoughts from a distance, rather than identifying with them, you create space between you and your thoughts. This shift helps you see them for what they are rather than absorbing them into yourself. Over time, this practice of separating yourself from your thoughts will help you notice a decline in their frequency. With practice and lots of patience, you may reach that state of no thought. No thought is a state where thoughts pass by, but you don't engage with them. It's a state of stillness where you are in pure awareness but free of any active thoughts. We may remain in the no-thought state for a short period, say a few seconds initially. Eventually, you can build on it. Remember, it takes patience and time.

Do not get worried if you cannot meditate for the first few times. Your mind may wander and travel to different places. Do not resist thoughts; instead, bring your attention back to breathing. You can express your thoughts like this, *'I acknowledge you, but now is not the time.'* Also, understand that it's not about perfection; it's about practicing it and looking into your inner self. Patience is your friend here. Some days, you would be able to feel deep and connected, while some days, you may find yourself distracted. It's okay. Over time, you will be able to master it.

There are different types of meditation, such as breath awareness meditation, leaves on a stream meditation, body scanning meditation, moonlight meditation, mindfulness meditation, and so on. Before we look at each of these, let us look at the preparations for meditating. Firstly, we need to identify a place where no interruption would occur. You can cleanse the house or the room you meditate by burning an incense stick or sage. While some recommend a specific location for meditation, others advocate for the freedom to meditate anywhere, anytime. As a beginner, it's beneficial to start with a consistent location to establish a routine. However, as you become more comfortable with meditation, you'll find that you can practice it in any setting. The key is to find what works best for you and to create a practice that fits into your life. Now, let's explore some meditation techniques.

Breathe awareness meditation

This is a simple yet powerful meditation. In this method, we pay attention to each inhale and exhale without controlling our breaths. Taking deep breaths will help you reduce stress, increase focus and concentration, and calm down.

The following are the steps for breathing awareness meditation:

- Find a comfortable position, either sitting or lying down.
- Close your eyes and take a few deep breaths.
- Focus on each inhale and exhale. Pay attention to your lungs expanding when inhaling and contracting when exhaling. Alternatively, you can focus on the air entering and leaving through your nostrils.
- If your mind starts to wander, do not resist; try to bring your focus back to your breath.
- Continue practicing for 5-10 minutes.
- Once done, open your eyes slowly.

Leaves on a stream meditation

In this meditation, you use a visualization technique to imagine a stream with leaves floating on it. These leaves represent worries, anxieties, and mental stress. You imagine your worries floating away from you by floating these leaves on the stream. This visualization meditation helps you release any emotional stress or anxiety.

Following are the steps for leaves on a stream meditation:

- Find a comfortable position, either sitting or lying down.
- Close your eyes and take a few deep breaths.
- Imagine yourself sitting beside a stream. Focus on the environment, whether you can see trees, whether it's a meadow, whether the water on the stream is cold, and so on. Try to visualize the details as much as you can.

- When a thought or a worry arises, imagine placing it on a leaf and letting it float away from you on the stream.
- Watch the leaf floating away from you and reach out of sight, meaning that your worries have disappeared from you.
- Continue this for each thought or worry that bothers you until you feel relaxed.
- Once done, open your eyes slowly.

Body scan meditation

Body scan meditation focuses on different body parts, from head to toe. This practice creates awareness of the body and helps release discomfort and physical tension. It also enables you to connect with the emotions hidden within the body.

Following are the steps for body scan meditation:

- Find a comfortable position, either sitting or lying down.
- Close your eyes and take a few deep breaths.
- Start by focusing on your toes. Notice if you feel any sensation like warmth or tension in that area.
- Slowly move on to your feet, lower legs, legs, and thighs individually and observe any sensation.
- Continue observing your upper body to your head.
- If you find any stress or uneasiness in any part of your body, relax that area. You can also send love and compassion to any part of your body experiencing stress.

- Continue this process for 10 to 20 minutes until you've scanned all your body parts.
- Once done, open your eyes slowly.

Moonlight meditation

Moonlight meditation offers a soothing experience as we meditate in the presence of the moon. If circumstances permit, you can practice this meditation outdoor. Otherwise, you can practice it indoors as well, gazing at the moon. If you practice it under a full moon, it is even powerful as the full moon's light is often associated with heightened energy and clarity. I often feel the calming energy of the full moon when I practice this meditation.

Following are the steps for moonlight meditation:

- Find a comfortable position, either sitting or lying down.
- You can keep your eyes open or closed in this meditation.
- Take a few deep breaths.
- You can look at the full moon and imagine receiving white light energy from the moon to you.
- Feel the energy touching you, calming and helping you release tension or stress.
- In every inhale, imagine you absorbing the positive, soothing energy from the moonlight, and in every exhale, release any stress or tension.
- Continue practicing for 5-10 minutes.
- Once done, open your eyes slowly and express gratitude.

Mindfulness meditation

In this meditation, we focus on the present moment:

- How you are feeling
- What thoughts you are getting
- What you are sensing without judging yourself

We often spend too much time solving problems, planning, or daydreaming, which consumes more energy than necessary. Fostering mindfulness helps us shift our attention away from these and focus on the present moment.

Following are the steps for mindfulness meditation:

- Find a comfortable position, either sitting or lying down.
- Keep your eyes closed.
- Take a few deep breaths.
- As thoughts arise, acknowledge them without judging and return to your present moment.
- You can also focus on the other senses, like smell, sound, and feelings. Simply watch them without judging.
- Continue practicing for 5-10 minutes.
- Once done, open your eyes slowly and express gratitude.

If you're a beginner and in the exploration phase, try out different meditations available online. I highly recommend starting with guided meditations, where you follow a voice prompt and practice along with it. Once you become comfortable, you can progress to no-thought meditations or explore other advanced techniques.

"Mental health is not a destination, but a process. It's about how you drive, not where you're going."

Noam Shpancer, PhD

Affirmations

Affirmations are positive statements repeatedly chanted by an individual to themselves to increase their confidence, shift their mindset to a more positive one, and reinforce positive beliefs. It is a powerful tool for reshaping our thoughts and beliefs. When repeated regularly, affirmations can help overcome negative self-talk and help cultivate a positive mindset. From personal experience, I've often found that what I affirm during my daily practice tends to manifest in my life. There have been many instances where things seemed to fall into place magically. Yet, I was also taking conscious steps towards my goals. Some things simply manifest at the right time, with the right opportunity. I believe that when you send a vibration or energy to the universe through affirmations, it responds to you, but only when it aligns with what's right for you and at the right time. I trust in divine timing, and I truly believe that affirmations help channel that energy, guiding the universe to bring the right things into your life when the moment is right.

Activity: Create Your Own Affirmations

In this activity, we'll explore some sample affirmations and guide you in creating personalised ones.

1. Sample affirmations:

Here are some examples to inspire you:

- I am worthy of love and respect.
- My potential is limitless.

- I trust in my abilities and decisions.
- I am capable of achieving my goals.
- I embrace challenges as opportunities for growth.
- Wherever I go, I prosper.

2. Create your own affirmations:

Follow the steps to create tailored affirmations that suit your life:

a) Find out areas of your life you want to improve.

b) Write empowering statements in the present tense.

c) Keep them short, specific, and meaningful to you.

d) Ensure they are achievable and reliable.

If you'd like free daily affirmations that I personally use, scan the QR code.

3. Your personalised affirmations:

Use this space to write affirmations that resonate with you:

1. ─────────────────────────────

2. ─────────────────────────────

3. ———————————————————————

4. ———————————————————————

5. ———————————————————————

6. ———————————————————————

7. ———————————————————————

8. ———————————————————————

9. ———————————————————————

10. ——————————————————————

4. Practice plan:

Decide when and how often you'll practice your affirmations. You can practice whenever you have time; there is no designated time for this. However, the best time to practice is in the morning when you wake up. That's when we are fresh and in a less cluttered state of mind. The more you practice, the better the results.

Affirmations are most effective when practiced in front of a mirror, like a self-talk exercise. If your morning routine does not allow time for affirmations, you can listen to them on YouTube or even create your own recordings. Simply record the affirmations in your voice and listen to them while driving or during stressful situations. Adding motivational music can enhance the effect of the recording. Just ensure you say the affirmations in a confident, empowering tone. This will instantly shift your mindset, bring peace, and create space for clear thinking, keeping self-sabotaging thoughts at bay.

Remember, regular practice and intense belief in the affirmations are the keys to shifting your thoughts to a powerful positive state.

Visualization

Visualization is one of my favorite techniques for bringing my goals and dreams into reality. It's like watching your dreams play out as a movie in your mind, reinforcing your belief in achieving the desired outcome. It is a technique where you imagine something you want to experience in every minute detail so that you unconsciously message your mind that it is possible and will work out for you. Through visualization, you are sending signals to your mind to prepare for the outcome of that visualization. It is similar to dreams, where you see visuals of someone or something. Here, you intentionally set the scene and visualize what you want to experience or achieve with the same intensity you would feel when it comes true.

Visualization is a powerful tool that can significantly boost your confidence. By visualizing your goals, you're not just focusing on the end result but also building the confidence and mental readiness to accept and feel worthy of the results. When you visualize big goals, such as building your first home, you're building your self-worth, signaling to the universe that you're ready to accept it without unworthy feelings or hesitation. This way, you're preparing your mind and body for the goal, telling yourself you can do this while fostering an optimistic approach and a strong sense of self-assurance.

How should you practice visualization? Let us start by identifying what you want to visualize. Choose one thing you would like to focus on before beginning the process. This is important because if you don't, there's a chance you may spend too much time deciding what to manifest, which could lead to distractions. Once you select a goal, find a quiet place to sit or lie down. I burn an incense stick or light a candle before visualizing to cleanse the area and create a positive atmosphere. Take a few deep breaths. Now, begin the visualization process. Suppose you have a job interview with your desired company next week and want to visualize its success. Start by imagining your entry into the office building. Observe the confidence in your body language—be proud of it. Then, picture yourself entering the office and meeting the receptionist. You're speaking to the receptionist, who asks you to wait. Within minutes, you're called in for the interview.

Visualize yourself confidently sitting across from the interviewer. How do you want the interview to unfold? Is it a one-on-one, a casual discussion, or a group interview? Set the tone. Picture yourself and the interviewer smiling, conversing easily, and shaking hands. You leave the office feeling happy and confident, certain you've secured the job because you sense it from the interviewer's demeanour. You return home and wait for the call.

I hope you understand the process I'm describing. Visualize every minute detail. This can work wonders.

Here are a few more tips: before you start visualizing, decide on small details such as your appearance, including clothes, accessories, and hairstyle. This way, you can already see the first steps of your visualization unfolding on your big day, just as you imagined. If you are presenting to a client, visit the room where you'll be presenting to understand what it looks like, where you will stand, and how many attendees there will be. This will help you set the tone to visualize with greater clarity. If you are going for a job interview, visit the building in advance. Decide how you will get there and locate the entrance. I visited my dream company several times before my interview. This gave me a sense of familiarity, and I could visualize myself going to the office daily. I used to take detours to pass the office or go for a random drive to my dream company, looking at the building and their logo. I would tell myself that I would soon be working there. This sort of self-talk and adding a touch of reality to your visualization dramatically helps. In this way, visualizing becomes easier because you are already familiar with the office logo, you've seen the building with your own eyes, and you've observed people coming and going. This is a powerful form of visualization where you physically experience the things you want most, helping you visualize with greater clarity and determination.

Similarly, you can visualize receiving an offer letter from the same company. Imagine getting a call from the interviewer or an email from the prospective employer. When you visualize, depending on your notification settings, you will get a notification on your mobile phone that displays the company's name. Visualize hearing the ringtone of the notification, then check your phone and swipe to look at the notification—there you go. You see an email from your dream company with the subject

"Congrats". Feel the happiness, jump out for joy, hug your partner or call your family to break the news. Feel the joy from your heart. Experience the happiness and the "I made it" feeling. Bringing these emotions, clarity, and minute detailing is essential as it works even faster when you visualize.

You can practice visualization in many ways—either by yourself or with the help of guided visualization videos and tutorials available on YouTube across various areas. You can visualize anything, whether it's career-related goals, relationship aspirations, financial success, or even a simple, happy, and slow-paced life. You can focus on visualizing one particular goal for a few days or switch between goals daily—it's entirely up to you.

I have created a playlist on YouTube for this purpose so I can choose a video based on my mood and desire to practice in the morning. This way, I don't spend too much time searching for the video. You can also practice it on your own if you prefer not to use guided videos. There are no fixed rules—it's all about imagination and gaining clarity.

Visualization doesn't mean you can skip effort and hard work; rather, it's a way of training your mind for success by focusing on the task and mentally experiencing the desired outcome.

Journaling Practices

Journaling is one of the simplest ways to capture your thoughts, emotions, and experiences. It serves as a tool for self-expression and self-discovery. When your mind is overwhelmed with negativity, journaling can help release stress and untangle those overwhelming thoughts. It allows you to analyse your feelings, understand their triggers, and develop healthier coping strategies. These reflections are key to lifting your mood and nurturing a stronger sense of self. The therapeutic nature of journaling can offer clarity, helping you navigate through challenging times.

To start journaling, set aside some time each day, preferably in the morning or before bed. Then, decide the medium- whether you're using free-style journaling or another method. If you're a beginner, you can use journals with prompts to help guide you as you get started. I have designed a collection of journals specifically for beginners. If you are interested in one, feel free to scan the QR code. I will also provide the details in the *'Tools and Resource'* section at the end of this book.

If you're free-styling, let the words flow without restriction. It will become a habit once you practice journaling at a specific time in your day. If you struggle to maintain consistency, I highly suggest incorporating journaling into one of your established habits, such as journaling while drinking your morning coffee. This way, you can practice consistently and maintain momentum. With regular practice, you'll be able to understand yourself better, improve your emotional awareness, and become a better being. It can motivate and commit you to your self-improvement journey.

There are many different methods of journaling. Following are some of the popular methods.

Gratitude journaling

Imagine starting your day with positive energy and appreciation. Rather than looking at the things you lack, you will focus on the things and people you have in your life. Isn't it wonderful to start your day by appreciating the little things you have and feeling happier because of it? By practicing gratitude, you will begin to look at life differently. You feel gratitude for small things that are present in your life that you haven't even noticed or appreciated before. You feel blessed, and joy becomes the norm in your life. It is natural for humans to focus on the problems; it is not straightforward for us to focus on the good as it takes effort, unlike problems. Looking at the blessings and appreciating the abundance will help you stay positive throughout the day.

When you write a gratitude journal, think about the people, things, circumstances, and surroundings you are grateful for. For instance,

- I am grateful for the cozy mattress that helps me get a good deep sleep.
- I am grateful that I get to spend money on my family.
- I am grateful for having a roof over me during the cold, providing warmth and shelter when I need it most.

Focus on the feelings and emotions rather than the writing. How you feel is what you feed to your mind and affect your subconscious.

Art journaling

Art journaling is a liberating form of self-expression that allows you to convey your feelings and emotions through visual art. Whether you're using craft papers, planners, fabric, stickers, clippings, or paintings, art journaling is about the joy of creating, not the perfection of the artwork. There are no set rules, so feel free to experiment and let your creativity flow.

To start art journalling, you must collect materials such as glue, art and craft supplies, scissors, sketch pens, etc. If you are new to this, many scrapbook cutouts and craft materials are available for online shopping. Having a space on the table to spread your craft items and move things around freely is also a good idea. Once you have done the preparations, you can think of the topic.

- How are you feeling today?
- What is the one thing that you want to focus on today?
- What are the things you are most grateful for?
- What are your inner strengths?

- What is your self-image?
- What does your ideal day look like?
- Messages for today?

You can choose a theme from the options above or select something else that comes to mind. Then, start organising your crafts that align with your theme. You can also write quotes, poems or messages using coloured pencils. Make sure to focus on the thoughts and feelings behind the artwork rather than on the polished result.

Free writing

Free writing is continuous writing without worrying about grammar or structure. You simply write down whatever comes to mind without pausing or correcting your sentences. This approach allows your thoughts to flow freely and helps stimulate creativity. To get started, you can use prompts like, *What am I feeling right now? What is bothering me now? What are my goals for today? What is something that has been on my mind lately?* Meditating or taking a few deep breaths beforehand can help you gain clarity and focus before diving into free writing.

Bullet journaling

Bullet journaling is well-structured and task-oriented, unlike other journaling approaches. Its primary purpose is to plan your daily, monthly, and future goals. You will jot down a detailed list of tasks, events, and notes using symbols known as signifiers for each month and day, aligning them with your future goals and dreams.

Following are the familiar signifiers used in bullet journalling:

- ● stands for tasks.
- - represents notes or thoughts. These are not tasks but just information that is good to note.
- 0 represents events or appointments.
- x denotes completed tasks.
- ✦ shows the task is of high priority.
- \> stands for tasks that are migrated from previous days to future days as they couldn't be completed.
- < denotes a specific task is scheduled for a future date in your calendar or future log.
- ? indicates the task requires additional clarification or research.

A bullet journal usually consists of an index of content with respective page numbers. Following the index, there will be a future log where you can log your long-term goals, events, and appointments against upcoming months. Next, you will have a monthly log. In the monthly log, you will have two parts: on one side, you will have a monthly calendar, and on the other, you will have a list of all the tasks assigned to that particular month. Once you complete the tasks from the right side of the tasks list, you can make notes on the calendar view against the day you completed them. Then, there will be a daily log where you list the tasks, events, and notes. This is the heart of the process, as you will rapidly add tasks as they occur. You can write down today's date, write down the task notes, and move on to tomorrow's date.

You can also create collections where you make a list of anything. It can come from your daily log, or you can start one anytime. For example, you could list the food you like, your hobbies, songs you like, places you like to visit, and so on. You can do many more things in a bullet journal, like mood trackers, habit trackers, mind maps, goal plans, and more. As I mentioned before, you can use a bullet journal to plan and organise anything in a structured manner. Creating a bullet journal lets you track your past, present, and future tasks, events, and thoughts in a single place. How good is that!

Reflective journaling

A reflective journal documents your thoughts, feelings, experiences, and reflections on those experiences. You look deep into yourself, analyse your feelings, and discover the triggers that caused you to feel this way. Then, you reflect on that experience, identify how you can improve and avoid such situations in the future, and the lessons learned. This process involves critical thinking and looking inside yourself to explore emotions and reasons. It also helps to self-explore and understand your core values and beliefs.

An example of a reflective journal could look like the following:

"*Today, I could not contribute anything to the client workshop. I felt frustrated that I didn't utter a single word. I focused more on my contribution than listening to the client and understanding their problems and concerns.*

Next time, I need to listen more without worrying about my contribution."

Journaling is a wonderful way to capture your thoughts, gain clarity, and explore yourself further. It doesn't matter which medium or method you choose— what matters is taking that first step.

"Life is 10% what happens to you and 90% how you react to it."

Charles R. Swindoll

Reconnecting with Nature

We lead fast-paced lives where connecting with Mother Nature has taken a back seat. It has become habitual for people to immerse themselves in smartphones, computer games, and digital platforms, leaving little thought for spending time outdoors. Nature plays a vital role in creating harmony in our mental health. This disconnection leads to numerous physical and psychological health issues, such as depression, stress, and anxiety. It also impacts physical health, causing a weakened immune system, obesity, and vitamin D deficiency. When we reconnect with nature and ground ourselves in it, many of these adverse effects can be reversed, helping us stay centred and mindful.

How can we stay connected to nature? Here are some ways to embrace your connection with nature:

- Take a daily walk in nature. If you do not have time, do a garden walk instead.
- Start gardening. Grow vegetables, flowers, and herbs, allowing you to connect to the cycle of planting, nurturing, and harvesting. By being involved in gardening, you get to explore many beneficial bugs and insects and invite more butterflies and dragonflies, thus transforming your place into heaven. I have a YouTube channel, *@TheUrbanGrowers*, where I share videos about starting a garden, easy DIY projects and educational knowledge about plants, chooks, bees and how to live a sustainable life.

- Grow indoor plants to improve air circulation and create a nature-inspired space within your home. I have more than 30 plants in my house, and they bring me an energy and positivity that words cannot fully describe. Many people worry about not knowing how to care for plants and may end up losing one or two. That's perfectly okay—learning from mistakes is part of the process and helps foster a genuine interest in nurturing them. Start with succulents or pothos, as they are very easy to grow. Over time, you'll discover which plants thrive in your care and which ones might be beyond your limits.
- Consider opening windows to let the light and air pass in and out of your house.
- If you exercise indoors, consider shifting one or two days to outdoors. You can go running in the nearby park or hiking or trail walking on the weekend to boost your connection with nature.
- Walking barefoot on natural surfaces has tremendous benefits. It allows you to absorb the earth's natural electrical charge, which is beneficial for our health. Earthing techniques also help increase blood flow in your feet and legs.
- Immerse yourself in the tranquillity of natural sounds like rain, bird songs, and buzzing of bees.

- Spend a weekend in your backyard, on a picnic mat, reading a book, or listening to nature. Grounding yourself in Mother Nature instantly boosts your energy and brings a sense of calm and peace.
- If you have spare time, you can volunteer at wildlife sanctuary or parks to help them maintain the area. It is a beautiful way to learn about nature while contributing to the community.
- Create a wildlife-friendly oasis in your garden, like a bird or bee bath. Enjoy the simple pleasure of watching birds, bees, and flies, sipping water, or bathing on a sunny afternoon. This not only entertains but also deepens your connection with nature.
- Go camping! It's a fantastic way to explore nature and reconnect with it. You can fully immerse yourself in nature and stay away from digital distractions, feeling the thrill of the unknown and the beauty of the natural world.

The energy you experience when you take a step closer to Mother Nature is simply amazing. It's a feeling that everyone should truly experience. It's pure, untainted love. Embrace the energy and love from nature, and share it with the world around you.

Digital Detox and Mindful Technology Use

Technology has made a massive impact on our well-being. It's high time we reflect on how it is affecting our mental health. Most of us work 9-5 jobs, spending hours in front of digital platforms. Once we're back from work, what do we do? We either spend time on our phones and laptops or watch Netflix. The time we spend in front of screens is significant—it's just that we don't realise it. It has become a habit to destress from work pressure by scrolling through social media or watching Netflix. Don't you think we're missing out on meaningful connections with our loved ones by not being fully present in the moment? Instead of cherishing those beautiful experiences together, we often find ourselves distracted. Don't you think we could truly listen when they're eager to share how their day went, rather than just hearing them passively? A simple smile or kind gesture could even create a wave of positivity, making our surroundings more beautiful and connected. Isn't it time to nurture these bonds and make the most of the time we have with one another?

But how can we create these beautiful memories and cherish these moments if we're continuously glued to our screens? Let's explore ways to embrace the mindful use of technology and make space for what truly matters. Here are some ways you can implement a digital detox.

- Take regular breaks from screens and connect with nature.
- Set reminders on social media so that you become aware of the time you're spending on it.
- Uninstall applications that you no longer use from your devices.
- Avoid using your smartphone or laptop at least one hour before going to bed.
- Turn off notifications on your devices; this will help avoid the temptation to check your phone constantly.

- You can add digital detox as a goal to your daily or monthly planner so that you get reminded of it every time you look at it.
- Find new hobbies or commitments and engage in them.
- Start building the habit of reading books. Reading not only reduces screen time but also improves focus and concentration. Read while travelling by train or bus, during leisure time, or before sleep.
- Writing is also a fantastic option. It helps to organise thoughts and reduce stress.
- Lastly, listen to your body; it knows better than your mind. If you feel tired of looking at screens, your eyes need rest, or your body shows signs of discomfort, take a break.

It's all about staying mindful and intentionally taking a pause. Eventually, this will become second nature, and you'll begin to find joy in nature, nurture relationships, and discover new hobbies. Start now!

Key Points to Remember

- Meditation is a wonderful practice that helps you to quiet your mind, monitor your thoughts and reconnect with your inner self.
- Detach from thoughts. The no-thought state is where thoughts pass by, but you don't engage with them. It's a state of stillness where you exist in pure awareness, free of active thoughts.
- Affirmations are powerful statements that you intentionally practice to overcome negative self-talk and cultivate a positive and confident outlook on life.
- Creating a visual image of your goals and dreams as if they have already been achieved is known as visualization. By visualizing the minute details of the scene of your desired outcome, you train your mind to believe it is possible and achievable.
- Journaling is a safe space to analyse your feelings, understand their triggers, and devise better coping strategies.
- Reconnecting with nature helps you experience a whole new world filled with positive energy, love, and compassion.
- Digital detox is about staying mindful of your use of digital technology and maintaining balance. Mindfulness is key to this practice.

4

Mastering Health and Fitness

Active living is a lifestyle choice that's as unique as you are. It's about integrating one or more physical activities into your daily routine. Whether it's brisk walking, running, playing sports, swimming, gardening, or cycling, you have the power to design your physical activity based on your interests and preferences. This control puts you in the driver's seat of your fitness journey, empowering you to make choices that suit your lifestyle and goals.

Importance of Active Living

Being physically active has numerous benefits. You may already know most of them, but sometimes, it doesn't fully register until you read or notice something that reinforces the idea. Staying active helps manage stress by releasing endorphins, which reduce anxiety and depression. Physical fitness also boosts self-esteem and gives you a sense of accomplishment, making you feel more confident and changing how you view yourself. People who exercise regularly or maintain an active lifestyle often experience increased energy levels, helping them stay productive and improve overall well-being. Additionally, it helps burn calories, maintain a healthy weight aligned with your BMI, and prevent health issues such as obesity and heart-related problems.

Staying physically active may sound easy, but it may not to some people, depending on their motivation and needs. Consistency is the key. Also, understanding why you want to incorporate this into your life will help you continue the journey. For some, it could be health; for some, it is an achievement; for others, it could be a stress buster. The first step is to identify why you want to incorporate physical activity into your life. Next, set your physical health goals by writing them down. What do you want to achieve through this—weight loss, muscle building, running for a specific duration, lean abs, or simply staying active? Once you have clear fitness goals, break them down into smaller, achievable steps. Each time you reach a milestone, you'll experience a sense of accomplishment that will keep you motivated and on track.

Suppose your goal is to build lean abs in twelve months.

1-3 months

Goal: Weight loss (fat) 2-4 kg;

- Incorporate beginner core exercise.
- Cut processed food items and reduce sugar intake.
- Healthy eating and staying hydrated.

4-6 months

Goal: Build muscles and burn fat

- Limit fast food.
- Add HIIT to your workouts.
- Start weightlifting based on health conditions; start with 1-2kg if you're a beginner.
- Eat healthy homemade food .
- Start visualizing your end goal.

7-9 months

Goal: Considerable loss in abs fat; visible 11 lines

- Focus on advanced core exercises like weighted planks, ab rollouts, etc.
- Incorporate an additional activity in the evening to burn calories. Even yoga or Pilates would be a good idea once or twice a week.
- Implement mindful eating. Stop when you feel 80% of your stomach is full.
- Visualize your goal and use positive affirmations.

10-12 months

Goal: Have lean abs

- Perform intense abs workout and HIIT.
- Fine-tune your routine to make it sustainable.
- Celebrate your wins.

Note: This workout plan is a sample. Please consult with a fitness professional or healthcare provider before starting any new exercise program to suit your individual health needs and fitness level.

By breaking down your goals, you gain clarity and a sense that it is easily achievable. Keep in mind that everyone has a unique lifestyle, health conditions, and preferences. The plan that works for me may not work for you, and you may need to consider creating one that suits you. You can start by creating a three-month fitness plan, and towards the end of three months, you can make the following plan for the next three months based on your progress. Sometimes, planning for too long may not work, as your circumstances and needs may have changed by then.

Activity: Create your own Active Living Plan

Main Goal :

_____

Subgoals: Break your main goal into smaller, actionable subgoals across the timeline.

Subgoal	Timeline	Action plan

Understanding the "Plateaus"

Do you feel like your hard work isn't paying off? Are your efforts not reflected in the results you expected? This phase is known as Plateaus. It happens when the progress slows down or even stops, even though your efforts are continuous. As far as you identify that you hit the Plateaus phase of your goal, you're good because awareness is the most important thing. There are many ways to overcome this phase, but what if you didn't even realise that this is what's happening to you in the current phase.

I often got stuck at this phase in my workout, and all I could see was that my results stayed the same despite my consistent workout and healthy eating. When I hit this phase of plateaus, I didn't realise what was happening. I made good progress but got stuck because I didn't see any visible changes and eventually lost motivation. This continued for a long time until I realised I was stuck in a loop. It was incredibly frustrating because I had to start from scratch every time. Each time I tried to lose weight, I hit a plateau phase where I didn't see any visible changes. I got demotivated, gained the weight back, and ended up repeating the cycle again. But once I became aware of this pattern, I felt empowered to make a change. As I said, awareness is the key here to overcoming this phase. How do you become aware of this? Just notice if you can relate to any of the following:

- You notice no significant change in weight or measurements or muscle building for several weeks.

- You feel demotivated to workout or stay active and struggle to stick to your plan.
- You feel uninterested in the same repeated routine/activities.
- You start to skip workouts or any form of physical activity that you've been doing.
- You begin to question whether it is making any impact and if it's worth continuing.

You might have hit the plateau phase if you see yourself going through any of these signs. This is quite a typical phase, especially when you try to implement some physical activity into your lifestyle. This is because your body adapted to this new activity you were trying to implement, making it less attractive as you have outgrown this situation. Listen to your body; if you need to try a different activity or increase intensity, do it. Introducing new things and styles keeps you excited and generates interest. For instance, if you have been doing the same exercise for 4 weeks, maybe try a new program or add up a few new workouts. If you have been practicing yoga for a while, try variations of yoga, like aerial yoga, power yoga, yoga nidra, or acro-yoga. The concept is simple: once you're bored and feel like you need a change, try different things or alter your program to bring some new excitement.

Sometimes, you feel Plateau because your nutrition plan needs revising. Making adjustments to your diet and nutrition is essential. Understanding the role of nutrition in your fitness journey can be a game-changer. Lastly, you might need to give your body more time to recover; hence, you feel sleepy and tired. Ensuring you have enough rest and recovery time on your daily schedule is essential. If you can't be flexible on weekdays, balance it during the weekend. You need to give enough time for your body to rest, recover, and reset to overcome the plateau phase.

The Importance of Breaks

Breaks are not a sign of weakness; they are a sign of wisdom. Regardless of the activities or tasks you are engaged in, taking a break is essential. It's the time for your body and soul to get enough rest, reflect and reset. Without adequate breaks, you start to burn out, and it will impact your thought process.

I was raised in a society where taking a break from something you continuously meant to do, say exercise or career, is not advisable. People are judged as lazy, inconsistent and demotivated. But life is tough, and you can't exist without a break; we humans need it. There is nothing wrong with taking a break from anything! Ultimately, it's all about doing what makes you happy and content.

Having a preplanned break is a great strategy. When creating an action plan for your active lifestyle or routine, include scheduled breaks. These give you something to look forward to and help keep you motivated. You could also plan a rest day on one of the weekends. Rest doesn't always mean staying at home; it could involve going for a massage, visiting a spa, or simply enjoying a beach day. These activities help recharge your energy. Remember, your body is your best guide—it knows when it needs a break. It's okay to take an extra break or adjust your planned one if your body signals that it needs rest.

"He who has health, has hope; and he who has hope, has everything."

— Thomas Carlyle

Healthy Eating

Often, people mistake healthy eating for following a strict diet. But it's about choosing the food mindfully that balances and nourishes your body and mind. Good food fuels your body with the energy, nutrients, and minerals required for well-being. Healthy eating is a vast topic and has many components. But I will pinpoint some of the elements that I think are important to look at:

- Limit the frequency of fast food eating; instead, try to cook food fresh. I am not suggesting here that you completely avoid food from restaurants. Everybody's situation will be different. Look at your lifestyle and see if there is a need for more home-based cooking.
- Include lots of vegetables and salads in your diet. Meal planning and preparation can effectively accomplish this. Every week, you can form a habit of creating a shopping list and ingredients for the next week's meal preparation. This way, you will have all the nutrient-rich food, which also helps reduce waste.
- Stay hydrated. Water is essential for maintaining energy levels and smooth digestion. If your water intake decreases over time, you may feel fatigued and have headaches. Carry a bottle of water with you if you can, or count how many glasses of water you drink. This way, you will be aware of your water intake. You can also consider taking short breaks at work to refill your water.

- Healthy food is not just about what you eat but also how it's prepared. The joy and love you infuse into your cooking can make a world of difference.
- A happy and positive cooking environment can make your food tastier. It also influences the mindset of the person cooking. If you cook with love, the food will be even more delicious. This is why moms' food always tastes so good: they cook with lots of love - a secret ingredient of the recipe!
- Refrain from regularly consuming lots of frozen food. I always felt the difference between cooking and eating fresh from the kitchen and the freezer! I hope you get it, too!
- It is essential to understand your eating practices. Even though you prepared nutrient-rich food at home, eating it fast just before a meeting without chewing properly will not do any good. Mindful eating involves paying attention to the food you eat, savoring each bite, and being aware of your body's hunger and fullness cues. Eating mindfully with respect while connecting to its taste and texture is magical. It will help you control your portions, as such food will fill your body and soul.
- Finally, taking a moment to be grateful for the food and the person who cooked it for us before consuming it can make a difference. It changes the way you look at the plate in front of you. There's a reason why people used to pray together as a family before consuming food. It's a practice that fosters appreciation and connection, making the meal more than just sustenance.

It may not make sense to everyone, but in the culture I come from, we value these little things from childhood. As a teenager, I hated following them, but now, revisiting them in adulthood, I've come to understand their value and significance.

The Importance of Sleep and Recovery

Having a good night's sleep for rest and recovery is as important as nutrition and exercise. Sleep helps boost mental health and ensures you're ready to restart tomorrow. Deep sleep is necessary for your body to bring clarity, improve your mood, and unlock your potential.

When you sleep at night, you will go through multiple rounds of sleep, known as sleep cycles. Each sleep cycle will have four stages, where 3 comprise Non-Rapid Eye Movement (NREM) and one REM. On average, a person goes through 4-6 sleep cycles. These sleep stages are critical as they help your body and brain to recuperate and develop. It will help you wake up feeling well-rested and refreshed. In other words, you should sleep well enough to build a lifestyle that supports your physical health.

What can disturb your sleep? Many things! Stress, anxiety, digital screens, and an unsuitable sleep environment can all interfere with your rest, preventing your sleep cycles from completing. Here are some suggestions from my experience to improve your sleep cycle:

- If you are going through stress or anxiety, consider writing a journal before you go to bed. By writing, you can unload everything bothering you into the journal, clearing some space and bringing peace to your mind.

- If you're someone who tends to overthink and finds that these thoughts disturb your sleep, try brain-dumping on a piece of paper. Write down anything that comes to mind to clear your thoughts and create space for restful sleep.
- Building a discipline around sleeping and waking time would be a good strategy. This way, you avoid shocking your brain by waking up at irregular times, such as waking up early one day and late the next.
- Creating a peaceful sleep environment can work wonders. Simple things like fresh bedsheets, a comfortable mattress, and a dimly lit quiet room can make a difference. And if you enjoy it, a hint of incense or a mild-scented candle can add a soothing touch to your sleep space.
- Here's a piece of advice you've probably heard before, but it's worth repeating: Avoid digital screens right before bedtime. The blue light emitted by screens can disrupt your sleep cycle, so giving yourself a screen-free buffer before you hit the hay is best.
- Avoid caffeine, alcohol, water, or even heavy meals close to bedtime. Caffeine keeps you awake, alcohol disrupts deep sleep, too much water may cause you to wake up for bathroom trips, and heavy meals can lead to discomfort. Limiting these before bed gives your body the best chance to stay asleep through the night.
- I like to pray and surrender everything to the universe before falling asleep. This way, I believe I am under

the universe's protection, and only divine energy can reach me.

I highly recommend observing your sleep patterns if you feel inactive and fatigued. According to research, adults typically require 7-9 hours of sleep to feel fully rested the following day. Remember, if you sleep well, you live well!

Key Points to Remember

- Staying physically active helps you manage stress by releasing endorphins, which, in turn, reduces anxiety and depression.
- Consistency is key. If you feel like you're hitting a plateau phase, make small changes to your routine. This can keep things interesting and push you forward.
- Taking breaks is essential; it gives your body and soul the time to rest, reflect, and reset, allowing you to recharge for better performance and well-being.
- Our food habits say a lot about our overall health. Consuming nutritious food nourishes not just your body but also your mind and soul, promoting well-being on all levels.
- Adults need an average of 6-8 hours of sleep to feel well-rested and energetic for the next day. A well-rested mind is a productive mind.
- Take care of your body, mind, and soul, and they'll take care of you.

5

Creating a Harmonious Home

Home is where we grow, learn, and evolve. As we say, a child's development depends on their parents and the family environment; the environment we create in a home also matters. There is a direct connection between the space you live in and your mind. A clean, positive environment creates clarity, peace of mind, and a sense of belongingness. When I was growing up, my parents were strict about keeping things in their place and staying organised. Like most teenagers, I didn't like it and didn't understand why it was so important. In fact, I often felt it was easier to find things when my room was a mess. But as I grew older, I began to realise how much easier my parents had made my life by instilling the habit of organisation and tidiness in me from a young age. I feel an instant sense of peace when I look around my home, no matter where because every space is neat and organised (except for my husband's shed, which I have no access to!). It's truly magical. After a rough day at the office, coming home feels so inviting and relaxing. The entire atmosphere lifts my energy and fills me with a sense of calm. This serene feeling is something you can only fully understand when you experience it in your own space. To those who already know what I mean—bravo, well done!

How you keep your home reflects your mental state. If you create a heaven in your place, you will most likely feel divine. The energy in the house would be so positive and uplifting that anyone who enters your home could feel it instantly. You feel so welcoming, positive, and happy in such places without even being aware of it. For instance, you might find yourself wanting to hang out at your friend's place because their home radiates a warm and inviting atmosphere. You may not consciously notice the energy or positivity in the house. But it creates an inner feeling that draws you in, making you want to spend time there and enjoy it fully. On the other side, have you ever had a situation where you visited someone's home, and you thought you wanted to go home as soon as possible? You don't feel like staying there, and you get so uncomfortable. It could be the smell, organisation of things, cleanliness, or energy stuck in the house. These good and bad vibes are based on how we transform a house into our home. It doesn't matter how small or old your space is; it's the environment you create in the house. Let's explore the transformative power of turning a house into a home full of good vibes, inspiring you to create your own positive sanctuary.

Keeping Your Home Clean and Organised

Imagine stepping into a clean and tidy home versus one cluttered, congested, and untidy. The difference in how you feel in these spaces is quite noticeable, and I'm sure you can sense it without further explanation. If you've become accustomed to the latter, it might be harder to recognise the clutter as you've grown comfortable in that environment. I hope this book inspires you to reflect and see things from a different perspective, helping you create the space that truly supports your well-being.

Declutter regularly

Decluttering your home is the process of clearing away things that are no longer needed. It's about creating more space by removing unnecessary things, from clothes to tools to toys. You might have accumulated stuff from your childhood without even realising it. I understand the memories and sentimental value they hold. Sometimes, it's about recognising that these items can make a difference to someone who needs them more than you do.

Take clothes, for example. You may have a favourite tee you bought two years ago, but sadly, it no longer fits. If someone who can wear it and is in need receives it, it becomes an incredibly thoughtful act. Similarly, as you look around your home, you may be surprised by how many such items you find—things that were once useful but no longer serve a purpose or are no longer usable, but you hesitate to discard. These small decluttering efforts can work wonders for your home.

To start decluttering, select area by area rather than just decluttering the whole house (as it could be cumbersome). If you are concerned that you might need to use an item in the next 6 months but not for now, then you can move it to your garage. If you don't use it in the next 6 months, it might be time to reassess the need. You can sell it in marketplaces or donate to salvos. My husband and I do this check every six months. If we haven't used an item in the past six months, we decide together whether to clear it from the house. You're not losing anything—in fact, you're helping someone else by donating it or selling it at a lower price. This process creates a sense of control and organisation over your living space.

The next question that comes to mind is, how often do you need to declutter? There is no right or wrong answer, it totally depends on your circumstances. I prefer to declutter every season. Once you do it initially, it becomes much easier, and subsequent sessions may only consume a little of your time. The pleasure you get from cleaning and clearing things off the shelves is fantastic. You will feel you have more space to breathe. The relief and freedom that come from decluttering are truly invigorating.

Establish cleaning routines

Cleaning the house can sound chaotic and troublesome. But if you change your perspective, it can be an enjoyable and deeply satisfying experience. Imagine a place full of dust and dirt and the feeling you get once it's clean and tidy! The sense of accomplishment is truly rewarding.

Depending on your needs and interests, you can clean your space daily, weekly, or monthly. I clean my house daily. However, detailed cleaning is done fortnightly or sometimes every month. If you see something unclean and clean it on the spot, you may have little to clean at the end of the day. A consistent cleaning routine can help you maintain your house without much stress.

You can start with a plan depending on how you approach this. List all the areas of your house that need regular cleaning. Then, identify weekly and monthly cleaning tasks to ensure everything is being cleaned. You might not even need a plan if you have a small to medium house that can be easily managed. You can clean the areas individually based on priority or require the most cleaning. But do it sparingly, as sometimes, it can be exhausting, too. Playing music or watching a movie you love while cleaning can be a great way to make the task more enjoyable, especially if you prefer not to fully immerse yourself in the cleaning process. Once you do it a few times, you'll quickly know where to focus more and what sort of cleaning is needed. This would make your life even better. But remember, don't be too hard on yourself if you happen to miss cleaning for a week or two; stay flexible when possible so that you can enjoy the process.

Maintain organisation systems

Have you ever felt like you just can't find something in the house when you need it? Or have you ever been so frustrated, thinking it was right there, only to realise it's nowhere to be found when you need it? If that's you, creating an organisation system may be a good solution. It's all about creating a system that works for you.

Begin by designating a specific place for things in your home. For instance, for all the stationary items, I have a separate container box with a name tag in it so that I know in which box I can find pens and pencils and in which box I can find glue and stickies. Let's say you struggle to find your car keys every time you leave the house. To tackle this, you can find a convenient place to hang your car keys. Make it a habit to hand it in the designated area. If you forget and bring it further along, consciously hang it back in the right place. And don't forget to appreciate yourself for the efforts you're putting in. It may seem small, but it's a lot of fighting and convincing that you're doing inside to come back and hang it at the right place.

To organise your entire space, I suggest tackling it area by area and deciding how you want to keep things organised in each section. Do you need containers? If so, what type would work best? Are organising accessories like bookends or stands necessary? Take the time to identify the materials you'll need to organise each area. This way, you can avoid delays by ordering them in advance and ensuring they're delivered when needed. If you love organising, take it as a project.

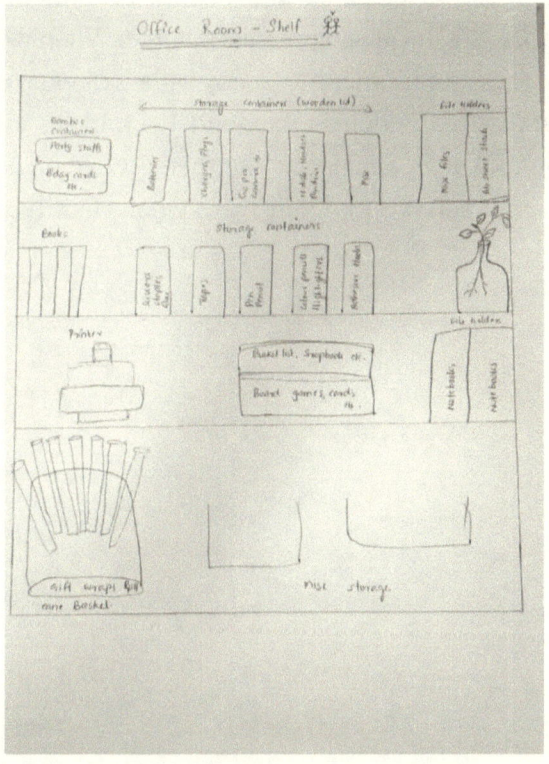

Picture of office shelf design

When we completed the settlement process for our first home, we were so excited to transform the space that we designed the shelves and racks before even getting the keys. We had a clear plan for what would go where on the shelves, including the arrangement of mirrors, decor, frames, and more. You can take this approach as far as you like, depending on your level of interest.

Putting things back in their proper place as soon as you notice they're out of place is also a great habit to develop. This way, you can avoid spending continuous hours cleaning and organising things. Also, involving everyone in your house in cleaning and organising will instil the importance of a clean and organised home. When we clean, we play music and sometimes enjoy a glass of wine or beer! We chat, dance, and clean together! It's fun! It's all about how you look at it. Changing your perspective on cleaning can become a fun activity for the whole family or as a couple.

Activity: 30-Day Decluttering Challenge

Declutter your home in 30 days, transforming it into a heavenly place. Focus on one area to start with and sort items based on *Keep, Donate, or Discard*. Here is a sample template to help you get started.

Day	Area to declutter	Task	Done?
1	Bedroom	Clear out clothes you no longer wear	Yes
2	Living Room	Sort through books and magazines	Yes
3	Kitchen	Declutter countertops and cabinets	In progress
4	Bathroom	Go through expired or unused toiletries	----
5	Office/Study	Organise paperwork and files	----
6	Closet	Donate shoes you don't wear	----
..			

If you'd like a free template to plan and execute your decluttering process, scan the QR code below to download your free copy.

"The magic thing about home is that it feels good to leave, and it feels even better to come back."

Wendy Wunder

Making Space for New Things

Who doesn't love shopping and bringing new things home? The question is, do we ever think about making space for new things? We often get so excited about new items that we forget to consider where to place them in our house. However, by following the '*one in, one out*' principle—where for every new item you bring in, one is donated, sold, or discarded—you can prevent clutter from building up over time. This helps you declutter your space while creating a more inspiring and motivating environment. While you may not always be able to apply this principle, being aware of it and keeping it in mind when you buy new things can bring a new perspective to your shopping habits.

Another effective way to make space for new things is through mindful acquisition. Before making a purchase, ask yourself, "*Do I really need this? Does it align with my values? Will it bring me joy?*" This habit not only encourages you to reconsider the item's value but also helps you fight impulse buying. By asking these questions, I've been able to bring home only the things that truly matter to me.

Boost Ambiance with Positive Elements

Indoor plants

Many of us have discovered the joy of bringing the outdoors in with indoor plants. The aesthetic they provide and the instant lift they give to a space are genuinely fascinating. They not only change the look and feel of a room but also nourish our eyes and instantly recharge us. I personally love the serene atmosphere my indoor plants create in our living room, giving it a mini forest look and a touch of nature's warmth.

Our living room filled with plants

Adding plants to your indoor space has many benefits. Do you know that they can influence our mood? When you enter a place with some greenery, it instantly makes you feel settled and peaceful. They improve the air quality by increasing the oxygen level, hence the name 'natural air purifiers.' Studies also say plants help reduce stress and anxiety and enhance productivity. Most workplaces have now incorporated more indoor plants in the work area; some even have a massive section for green plants. Plants are believed to improve concentration and boost creativity, making you a superstar at work! Beyond all of the above, plants help us stay connected to nature, even when living in urban areas or small spaces. If you have little or no backyard, I recommend introducing some indoor plants to your space. Watch yourself the magic they do.

Choosing the right plant for you and your space is very important. If you are a beginner, start with one or two plants. Buying all the big, beautiful plants you see at the nursery is exciting, but I suggest taking it slow. Starting with a few plants will help you understand if you have a genuine interest in growing and caring for them. Plants are like little babies who need our attention. They are dependent on us. Having that commitment is quite essential. Next, watch the space to see how much filtered light your room gets where you plan to place the plant. Natural light is essential for the growth of plants, and based on the amount of light you receive in your area, you can choose plants. If your space receives a lot of indirect sunlight, plants like monstera, various types of pothos, bird of paradise, and fiddle leaf fig are great options. For areas with less than moderate sunlight, consider ZZ and snake plants. Always do your research before bringing a plant home.

When it comes to plant care, ensure you water them regularly, keeping in mind that each plant has different requirements. For example, snake plants dislike overwatering, so a fortnightly watering routine works well. In contrast, Monsteras and Pothos prefer to retain some moisture, so watering once or twice a week may be ideal, depending on your region and humidity levels. When it comes to fertilising, you can think of it as food. Without food, they would not survive like us. You can go for solid or liquid fertilisers based on your suitability. If you live in a dry region, using a humidifier will benefit your plants, as they thrive in humidity. I recommend occasionally keeping them under the shower for a nice bath to energise and get a fresh feel. You can wipe the leaves afterwards, which would remove any dust particles sticking to their leaves.

Lighting

Incorporating string lights or twinkle lights is an excellent idea to elevate the ambience of your space, especially in the evenings. There is something special about their glow—they are so melting, and you instantly feel relaxed and cozy. We have different types of string and LED lights in each area of our home, adjusting them to suit the mood. The ambiance these lights create is simply amazing. Plus, they're energy-efficient too! If you want to enhance the aesthetics of a space and improve the mood, then LED string lights are a game changer.

The use of candles is another excellent idea. Our winter nights feel incomplete without the warmth and glow of a candle. The ambience it brings and how it lights up a room is fantastic. It is perfect for relaxation and uplifting your mood. You get a wide range of candles, from paraffin to soy to beeswax candles, in different shapes, sizes, and scents. Lighting them during dinner creates a wonderful atmosphere. And it doesn't always need to be a romantic couple dinner; you can set the dining for yourself—just a little treat for you for all the excellent work you're keeping up. I enjoy lighting a candle with my twinkle lights, playing music, and enjoying every bite of my food. It's a gift I give to myself during long, hard days. If interested, check out our *@enchantedcandlesbyns* on Instagram for some excellent scented soy wax candles.

ENCHANTEDCANDLESBYNS

Mirrors

Mirrors are often overlooked when designing a space. It is an element that helps to elevate the ambience of your space. It reflects natural light and helps brighten the space, making it look more spacious and open. Different styles of mirrors are available in the market, from minimalistic to decorative mirrors. Based on the style of your home, you can choose suitable ones. You can keep them in the entryways, hallways, living rooms, or bedrooms to create an aesthetic appeal.

Incense

Incense is something that I can't live with. The magic that it does in my house is simply amazing. When you burn an incense stick, it instantly uplifts the mood in that space. It calms you down with the gentle aroma, helping you relax. If you practice meditation or yoga, use an incense stick of your favourite scent. It can enhance your focus while fostering a deeper spiritual connection. Every morning, I burn one or more incense in my house and move it to every part of my house. In many traditions, it is not just a sensory experience but symbolises rituals. It is believed to cleanse the space, dispel negative or unwanted energy, and invite more positivity into your house. This is considered to be part of purification.

Crystals

Crystals are believed to emit positive energy, transforming the space into a balanced and harmonious environment. There is a huge variety of crystals, and each comes with a different purpose. For instance, rose quartz promotes self-love, amethyst for calmness and spiritual connection, and selenite for cleansing and clarity. If you feel attracted to crystals, research and understand their importance and how to cleanse, charge, and set intentions on them. Ultimately, it's a calling. If you feel like being called to use a crystal or attracted to it, it's a sign - go for it. Crystals can be seen as energy carriers that help balance the energy in a space, cleanse negative energy, and bring greater clarity.

Create Functional Spaces

Designing a functional space in your home is essential for both organisation and comfort, especially when living in a small, compact space. Whether it's for work, relaxation, games, or meditation, create a designated space for this. This way, you can design your space by utilising every part of it to meet your needs. Plus, your brain gets a signal that this is what you intend to do when you sit in a designated area. It helps to build a mental association and enables you to focus more. For instance, we have an office room with two desks and screens, which was primarily used for work. This space gave us the sense that, by 7 a.m., we knew exactly where to go, and our brains automatically adjusted to the work environment. Later, when I needed to incorporate a meditation area, I rearranged the office room in such a way that I got a separation from my office desks and screens while enjoying a space for myself just for meditation. Creating a functional space for important activities would help you mentally prepare and focus more. But stay flexible and be open to arranging and rearranging as your needs evolve!

New meditation space in our office room

Maintaining a Harmonious Home

Now that we've learned how to create a harmonious home, let's talk about maintaining it. The good news is, it's simpler than you think. Just continue implementing the strategies you've learned on a regular basis. If you're new to this, you can even create a tracker to monitor your progress. The key is to allow yourself to continue these practices, as they contribute to mental and physical clarity and peace. Don't be shy to add or remove items from your home based on your mood and interests.

You can also consider a seasonal refresh and update for your house if you're keen. For instance, in winter, you might use many strings of lights, candles, and cosy throws. After the season, you can store them in an organising container, making space for new items for the next season. This way, you do not clutter a space. Try rearranging, clearing, and storing things rather than keeping everything together. If you take an item onto your shelf, take one thing out; remember the One-In, One-Out Rule.

Key Points to Remember

- There is a direct connection between the space you live in and your mind. A clean, positive environment creates clarity, peace of mind, and a sense of belongingness. A tidy home is often a sign of a happy and healthy family.
- Practice decluttering regularly. It clears your mind, creating space for new things while allowing energy to flow into your space.
- Apply the "one in, one out" principle, whenever possible. For every new item you bring into your home, donate, sell, or discard one. This helps prevent clutter from building up over time.
- Elements like indoor plants, twinkle lights, open windows, and incense can enhance the aesthetic appeal and atmosphere of your space.
- Functional spaces are important as they help your mind set the intention and mood, preparing you for tasks with full focus.

6
Cultivating Wealth Mindset

A wealth mindset is not about how much you earn or your bank balance; it's the lens through which you see wealth, how you think about it, and the choices you make. A common misconception about wealth is that it's solely about money, but this doesn't capture its full essence. Wealth can be any asset and resource, including money, that contributes to one's prosperity. On a different glass pane, wealth can also be defined in intangible aspects like experiences, the knowledge you build, and relationships. It is a culmination of both tangible and intangible elements. The definition varies based on people and their perceptions. Still, for me, it is a balance of financial, mental, and emotional well-being. However, an important part of wealth management is how we think about money. Money is a medium that helps us experience things and brings security to our lives. After all, we all need money.

Shifting Your Money Mindset

Let's start with an activity. Close your eyes and take a few breaths. Now, think of money. Write below the images, emotions, experiences, and thoughts that come to your mind. Let it be spontaneous; do not limit or restrict any words—just let them flow. This activity is designed to help you understand your current money mindset and begin the process of shifting to a wealth mindset.

Your thoughts might include abundance, sadness, lottery, worries, people's faces, experiences, beliefs, hard work, purse, shopping, the pain of spending money, the emotions when money credits to your account, fear of overspending, liabilities, salary increments, and so on. Once you've noted everything down, take a moment to reflect. Ask yourself: is the majority of what you noted positive or negative? What is the overall energy you associate with money? This reflection will help you understand your current relationship with money and the type of energy you're releasing toward it.

The relationship you build with money is quite essential. Money is energy, even though people mainly consider money to be physical notes or coins. Have you ever heard anyone say there is a physical shortage of money in the world or there isn't enough physical money for everyone to use? Not really. There is no scarcity of money in the form of cash or coins. Money itself is not scarce; it's abundant in the world. It's free-flowing. But why do we often complain that we don't have enough money? Is that the belief you hold about money and the energy you're putting out into the world—that you don't have enough? If that's the case, how can you expect to receive abundance? Remember, what you give is what you get, and this is why I said money is energy.

If you keep thinking that you struggle to make money and that money doesn't come easily to you, that's the natural vibe you're projecting. However, if you shift this mindset in your favour, magic can happen. Think of it this way: nothing good can flow your way if you view money in a negative light. So, what's the harm in adopting a positive mindset and experiencing the difference?

"Money is a living entity, and it responds to energy exactly the same way you do. It is drawn to those who welcome it, those who respect it."

                                    Suze Orman

Steps To Overcome Money Energy Block

I understand it's not easy to question the beliefs you have been trusting for these many years and tell your brain they're wrong. Remember, it's a gradual process, and you can take it step by step. Be patient with yourself as you navigate this journey of self-discovery and financial awareness.

The first step is to become keenly aware of the money energy and money blocks you may have. These blocks might not exist in all areas of your financial life. For some, they arise when spending; for others, when thinking about future security, or perhaps when asking for or receiving money. This self-awareness is the first step toward taking control of your money blocks. The following list outlines scenarios that can help identify areas where you might have money blocks. These are the starting points for working toward personal growth and financial well-being.

- You feel like you don't have enough
- You look at a wealthy family and think rich people are no good
- You feel anger when you need to pay tax
- You feel jealous looking at people who are prosperous and wealthy
- You feel uncomfortable when you receive unexpected money
- You feel guilty when you spend money on yourself
- You believe money is the root cause of all the evil

- You feel stressed when looking at your bank balance
- You avoid passive incomes, worrying about how to handle it
- You worry too much about losing money
- You believe you will never be rich as it's not achievable in this lifetime
- You feel uncomfortable when giving or receiving gifts
- You strongly believe you need to work hard to earn money
- Fear of being judged when you make less or more money
- Earning more could result in people asking you for help

The next step is to be aware of your emotions every time you encounter triggers around money blocks. For instance, suppose you have a money block when you spend. Let's say your car needs some TLC, costing you a couple of thousand dollars—how do you feel? Is it positive or negative? Change the emotions around any spending to a positive one. Because what you give is what you attract. Spend happily. Bless the money and tell it to help the community and make a positive impact. Spend it wholeheartedly, trusting it will return to you as double the amount. Change your attitude and thought process. By doing this, you're shifting your money energy and attracting money instead of repelling it.

I understand it takes a lot of internal effort because you're questioning long-held beliefs and rewiring your thinking process. But let me ask you this: what do you have to lose by adopting this mindset? Absolutely nothing! On the other hand, by redirecting your energy toward money with positivity, you might gain a fresh perspective—one you never imagined possible.

Activity: Transform Your Money Mindset

Here's an activity that will guide you in identifying your positive and negative beliefs about money. This step is a crucial part of your personal development journey, helping you build a healthier relationship with money. Following is a template that empowers you to transform your negative beliefs about money into positive ones. This process puts you in control of your financial mindset and motivates you to make positive changes.

Step 1: Identify negative beliefs

List your false beliefs about money and wealth. For example:

- "Money is not good for family relationships."
- "Money is evil"
- "Money makes people greedy."
- "Money brings problems."
- "Money is pain."

Step 2: Transform your negative belief into a positive belief

For each negative belief, write a corresponding positive statement.

Step 3: Justify the positive belief

For each positive belief, provide evidence, experiences, or justification. This will reassure you and boost your confidence, helping your conscious mind accept it.

Step 4: Action plan

For each positive belief, write down at least one action you can take to reinforce it. This will give you clear direction and a sense of determination to turn your beliefs into reality.

False belief	Positive belief	Justification	Action
e.g.: Money is a pain	Money is an empowerment.	- I used money to help those in need. - People make donations to charities to uplift our communities.	Each morning, I will stand in front of the mirror and repeat a money affirmation 5 times with complete trust.

Money affirmations

If you want to take your money energy to the next level, you can practice the following affirmations daily. Affirmations will help you reinforce your positive beliefs and shift your mindset positively. It is good to inject these powerful affirmations in the morning so that the thoughts and images you input into your mind are positive.

- I am a money magnet, and I make money easily
- I am financially free
- I am worthy of financial abundance
- Money comes to me quickly and effortlessly
- I am attracting more and more money every day
- My income is increasing constantly
- I earn $X.00 every month easily and effortlessly
- Wherever I go, I prosper
- Every dollar I spend comes back to me in double
- I have more than X (number) passive income sources
- I am in control of my money
- I am open to receiving unexpected wealth
- I release all resistance to attracting money
- I welcome abundance into my life
- I am confident in my financial future
- I am grateful for all the abundance I have and the abundance that is on its way.

Ho'oponopono

Ho'oponopono, an ancient Hawaiian practice, is a transformative journey of healing and building harmony within oneself. By chanting this prayer to clear your money blocks, you can begin to shift your relationship with money. As you chant, focus on the intention of releasing blocks and false beliefs around money and opening yourself to abundance.

You start this practice by saying, "I *take full responsibility for this negative experience or emotion happening to me*," and then repeat the following:

- *"I am sorry."*
- *"Please forgive me."*
- *"Thank you."*
- *"I love you."*

You can repeat this prayer until you feel content and peaceful. It is believed that Ho'oponopono prayer is so powerful that it can help heal your emotions and give you mental clarity. It helps to embrace inner peace by encouraging forgiveness to self and others. If you're new to Ho'oponopono, there are numerous videos on YouTube that can guide you through the practice. Feel free to explore and deepen your understanding.

Budgeting Fundamentals

Budgeting is a powerful tool that empowers you to take control of your financial stability. It's about allocating your income to different categories and aligning your spending with your values and goals. By implementing a budget, you ensure your essentials are covered while allowing for some flexibility for miscellaneous expenses. Budgeting has numerous benefits, from making informed decisions to reducing stress to bringing clarity to your finances.

There are many theories for following the budget process, but my favourite is the 50/30/20 rule. It's simple: 50% of your income goes toward essentials like mortgage, utilities, transportation, insurance, and groceries. 30% of your income is allocated to wants, such as travel, vacations, dining out, leisure, and hobbies. The remaining 20% is for savings, investments, and extra debt repayment. This method is popular because it balances income and expenditure effectively. However, how you allocate your budget depends on your lifestyle, income, and priorities. If you can save an additional 10% from the second category, you can add it to your savings budget. The flexibility allows you to adapt the method to what works best for you.

Regardless of the budgeting method you choose, I strongly recommend prioritising savings. By allocating the 20% to savings first, you ensure you never compromise on financial security or additional repayments. There are also many online tools available to digitalise your budget, making it easier to track savings and expenses.

Budget tracker template

Here is a simple budget tracker template that you can use to list your budget against your income. Under income, record all your monthly earnings. Under budget, assign your allocated amounts for each category. As the days progress, you can update the actual amount and if there is any difference between the two. This way, you can track where to improve next month and consider those adjustments.

Category	Allocated amount ($)	Actual amount ($)	Gaps/differences ($)	Notes
Income				
Salary				
Other income				
Total Income				
Budget				
Needs (50%)				
Rent/mortgage				
Utilities				
Transportation				
Groceries				
Misc				

Category	Allocated amount ($)	Actual amount ($)	Gaps/differences ($)	Notes
Wants (30%)				
Restaurants				
Shopping				
Hobbies				
Misc				
Savings (20%)				
Super annuation				
Investments				
Extra debt repayment				
Other savings				

Expense Management

Managing your expenses is a key to financial freedom and stability. It's not just about cutting costs but also about the empowering decisions you make with your money. It gives you the power to understand and control where your money is going. While a budget sets spending limits in advance, expense management puts you in the driver's seat, allowing you to monitor your real-time spending and make adjustments to stay within your budget. For example, if you set a $500.00 monthly budget for groceries, expense management will help you track your spending against this limit. This not only helps you stay within your budget but also gives you a sense of accomplishment when you reach the end of the month without overspending.

The following is a sample monthly expense tracker.

Expense	Amount	Income	Amount
Rent/mortgage		Individual 1	
Credit card repayment		Individual 2	
Internet bill		Additional	
Water bill		**Total income**	$
Energy bill			
Gas bill			
Vehicle rego			
Phone			
Subscriptions			

Grocery			
Transportation			
Self-care			
Fuel			
..			
..			
..			
Misc			
Total expense	$		
Savings (Total income - Total expense)	$		

If you want to understand where your money is going, analyse your expenses at least once a week. This way, you can adjust your monthly payments to align with the budget, even if unforeseen expenses occur.

Strategies to reduce expenses

Here are some strategies to reduce your monthly expenses:

- Distinguish between your wants and needs. This doesn't mean completely ignoring your wants, but understanding what is required at the moment will help you manage expenses better. Remember our 50/30/20 rule: you still get to spend 30% on wants.

- When planning your budget, it's crucial to be realistic and base your expenses on your income. This approach will reassure you that you're making sound financial decisions.
- Review your subscription list. It would be surprising to know that some silly amount is going towards a subscription you don't need to use. Every dollar saved is a dollar earned.
- Depending on your circumstances, cook from home if you can. Plan how many dining out you can afford and prepare food at home accordingly.
- Save energy by turning off unused lights or unplugging devices. Switching to low-voltage, energy-consuming appliances is also a good idea.
- I often find that the rates for mobile plans, internet plans, and insurance providers change every year. It is a good idea to check with other providers and see if you can get a better package for less money.
- Set up an auto transfer from your account to your savings account on a specific date each month so that you consistently save a particular amount without even thinking. This way, you will have to manage your expenses with the remaining balance amount.

Debt Management Strategies

Most of us are in some form of debt, whether an education loan, house loan, car loan, or some other sort. Debt has become part of our lives, defining our ways of living. Now, the point is to manage debt in a healthier fashion. There are a few strategies that you can consider to manage debt better.

- Prioritise debt payment by setting auto transfer. This way, you make sure the payments are made without any failure.
- Make an additional repayment every week or fortnightly. The expense tracker would help you here immensely. If you find out that one of the utility bills is not as high as expected, you can have the balance amount from the budget to the mortgage repayment. This would be an additional amount you would be paying on top of monthly repayment.
- Mortgage tracker: Create a spreadsheet tracker and see the amount you are paying now and when you will finish your mortgage. Adjust the interest rate slightly, as there will be fluctuations yearly based on your plan. If you can add a lump sum amount every year or an additional repayment every month, you can add it, too. This way, you will understand the earliest time you will be able to finish your mortgage. This will give you clarity and a vision for your future. Plus, it is a motivational boost to finish it earlier.
- Once you know the approximate year you will be finishing your mortgage, if you like, you can visualise the feeling of being mortgage-free. Experience freedom. Would you laugh and be happy? What would you do? How would you feel about it? Just close your eyes and feel it. This visualisation will help you manifest your goal even faster. There are many visualisation videos on YouTube related to money

and mortgages. You can check them out if you want to try them.

- We use a doodle tracker to monitor every additional $100 we pay. We contribute an extra $10,000 each year. Every time we transfer $100 to our bank account, we colour a doodle. If we transfer $1,000 at once, we get to colour ten doodles. This has become a couple's activity for us, as we enjoy seeing whose doodle turns out the cutest among the ten. Sticking the tracker somewhere visible, like the kitchen rack or fridge, helps us notice it often and encourages the habit of making additional payments regularly.

Tiny doodles illustrating additional repayments.

If you'd like a free template to help you get started with the debt repayment process, scan the QR code below.

We also have a *Mortgage Pay-off Tracker* book available on Amazon that you can use to track your repayments with cute doodles and other fun shapes.

- Instead of paying a mortgage every month, if you change it to a fortnight, you will pay an extra amount without even noticing much difference. If you have a monthly schedule, you will pay 12 payments in a year. If you pay fortnightly, you will pay 26 fortnights (52 weeks total), meaning 13 whole payments.
- Enquire other banking institutions for a better interest rate. Sometimes, you will find good packages where you get some lump sum amount from the bank to

change your mortgage to their account. Who doesn't love extra money?

- If you use an offset account for your mortgage and a credit card for all your expenses, your bank account retains funds for up to 45 days, reducing the interest on your loan. You will be using your credit card for regular expenses, and the credit card allows you 45 days to repay without any charges. The amount you spend on the credit card stays in your offset account, thus reducing the mortgage interest you pay.
- Affirmations play a big role in keeping you positive and determined. You can customise your own affirmations or use the list I shared before. You can even record them in your voice and listen to them every day. It's a game changer as it helps instil the mindset and emotions of being mortgage-free, reinforcing your focus and motivation.
- Avoiding new debts is a good consideration so you can focus on one mortgage repayment and finish soon. This will give you some sense of achievement!

Financial Goal Setting

Goal setting is key to achieving financial freedom and independence. By clearly defining your goals, you signal your brain to focus on achieving them. Writing them down as SMART goals creates a mental mindset that naturally aligns with your thoughts and actions. For example, a financial SMART goal could be: "I want to save $10,000.00 by December 2025." Here, you are specific about what you want to achieve: saving $10,000.00. You can measure this goal by tracking your savings progress every fortnight or month. It is achievable with lifestyle adjustments and your current earnings. The goal is relevant, as savings contribute to financial security and priorities. Since the goal includes a deadline, it is also time-bound.

When identifying your financial goals, consider what financial freedom means to you. For some, it may mean luxury; for others, it could be travel or being debt-free. Once you've defined your version of financial freedom, write down your short-term, mid-term, and long-term goals. For example, paying off credit card debt in the next three months could be a short-term goal. Saving 10% for your first home deposit within the next two years might be a mid-term goal. Paying off your mortgage entirely in the next 6–10 years could serve as a long-term goal.

Once you identify your goals, break them into smaller tasks and assign a realistic deadline. For example, if your goal is to pay off all your credit card bills in the next three months, you can further break it down into the following tasks:

- Assess your financial situation, including calculating total debt.
- Cut back expenses where possible in the next 3 months and repay the savings.
- Increase income by taking a freelance job or taking up gigs.
- Pay 50% of credit card debt.
- Pay 100% credit card debt.
- Cancel your credit card.

This way, you have full clarity of the tasks you want to achieve to reach your final goal. Similarly, you can break down your long-term goals. Monitoring and tracking your financial goals helps you take ownership of them and make meaningful progress. As you achieve these goals, you will experience a sense of accomplishment that will motivate you to continue working towards your financial independence.

Building Multiple Income Streams

There are several ways to increase your income, both passive and active. Passive income is earned consistently without continuous effort, while active income is earned by exchanging your time and effort, such as a salary. Passive income may require some initial capital, but once established, it generates ongoing returns. By diversifying your income streams, you not only grow your wealth but also free yourself from the constraints of a 9-5 job, giving you the freedom to shape your financial future.

Here are some guidelines for building multiple income streams.

- Identify the income sources that align with your skills and interests.
- Assess the practicality of the identified income sources—ask questions like whether it is in your genuine interest, how long you would be able to pursue this, what the positives and negatives are, etc.
- Start small. In the beginning, we will have lots of energy and enthusiasm to start and experiment, but

eventually, some of it will drop. Starting with one or two streams would be a good strategy. This way, you can balance your lifestyle and not feel overwhelmed by the process.
- Do your research—understand what to expect and what the worst thing that could happen is. This way, you can better handle the situations.
- Try to reinvest your earnings from an investment whenever possible. This way, you can grow your investment profile without you knowing it.
- Use trial and error to determine what works for you and what does not. Do not be afraid to try new things. Remember, you learn only when you try things. Mistakes are not failures but rather excellent lessons for growth and development, leading you to new and better opportunities.
- Regularly analyse your financial performance, thus allowing you to adjust your strategy.

There are several income sources that allow you to build passive income based on your interests, skills, and experience. Identifying the right one for you will be the key to your financial success.

Activity: Passive Income Ideas

Here is an activity designed to identify and pick income sources that may suit your interest. Again, ensure that you choose one based on your lifestyle.

a) Read through the list of 50 passive income ideas. Circle 5 ideas that interest you most.

List of passive income sources

1. Market shares
2. Stock market dividends
3. Mutual funds
4. Exchange Traded Funds (ETF)
5. Government bonds
6. Fixed deposits with high-yielding interest rates
7. Investment in commodities like gold, silver
8. Real estate sell and buy
9. Rent out your real estate properties
10. Lease your land
11. Beekeeping for honey
12. Free-range eggs
13. Rent out a spare room
14. Start a franchise
15. Rent out event supplies
16. Rent out campervans or caravans
17. Rent out trailers
18. Rent out kayaks, bicycles, or scooters
19. Sell painted pots and containers

20. Sell at local Sunday markets
21. Create and sell online courses
22. Write and sell eBooks
23. Sell handcrafted items on Etsy or Amazon Handmade
24. Sell stock photos or videos
25. Sell digital templates on Etsy or Amazon
26. Consulting in your area of expertise
27. Sell home-made products
28. Sell your cookbooks
29. Sell read books on marketplaces
30. Editing and proofreading gigs
31. Online marketing
32. Design and sell KDP (Kindle Direct Publishing) books on Amazon
33. Start Amazon Associates (affiliate marketing)
34. Host online workshops in your area of expertise
35. Publish crosswords or puzzle books
36. Rent out digital devices like drones, gaming consoles

37. Start a side hustle like garden designing or soap making

38. Freelancing (e.g., graphic design, content editor gigs)

39. Offer graphic designs like logos, banners

40. Online or in-person tutoring

41. Babysitting or pet sitting

42. Sell used items on marketplaces

43. Propagate indoor plants and sell them on marketplaces

44. Sell plants, seedlings, or seeds

45. Sell compost

46. Sell worm tea

47. Sell firewood

48. Sell fresh produce from your garden

49. Landscape designing

50. Start a YouTube channel and monetise

b) Evaluate each of your five chosen ideas, and answer: *"Why do I like this idea?"*, *"What skills do I already have for this?"*, and *"What and when would I need to start?"*

c) Now, choose your top one from the list of five.

_____

d) List 3 steps to get started on the top idea you selected.

   1. _____

   2. _____

   3. _____

e) Choose one small step you can take in the next week to start exploring your favorite passive income idea.

   _____

   Timeframe: _____

Financial Education and Literacy

Financial education from childhood is crucial for building money habits, managing personal finances, and making informed decisions about investments and saving. Beyond that, understanding the value of money and the comfort it provides is something one must learn through personal experiences. I grew up with little to no knowledge of finance, and it took me a long time to grasp the concepts and strategies related to money. But it's never too late! That financial knowledge has helped me shape my present and future in ways I once only dreamed of. It transformed my relationship with money from casual spending to mindful and respectful spending. I used to approach money with an attitude of taking it for granted, but gaining financial knowledge taught me to view it differently—with love, respect, and appreciation.

Several books talk about finance management and are readily available for anyone wanting to learn. If you are a reading person, you can get started from there. Podcasts are another great way to learn about money and wealth, and you can access them easily through various platforms like Spotify, Audible, Google Podcasts, and Apple podcasts. Online course platforms like Udemy are great for building insights into financial matters and understanding strategies, and they are just a click away.

Remember, when it comes to financial education, it's not just about understanding the financial terminologies and concepts; it is also an energy. If you know it from both these perspectives, it can take you a notch ahead.

Key Points to Remember

- Money is energy, and the relationship you build with it is essential. How you perceive and interact with money can greatly influence your financial success.
- Self-reflection on money blocks is crucial. By being aware of your emotions and the triggers behind them, you can shift negative feelings into positive ones and overcome any limiting beliefs you may have.
- Tools like affirmations and the Ho'oponopono prayer are excellent resources for working on your money energy and removing any blocks. These practices can help you cultivate a more positive mindset towards wealth.
- Budgeting and expense management are key to financial stability. By managing your finances efficiently, you gain a clearer understanding of your cash flow, allowing you to save more and make informed financial decisions.
- Financial goal setting is just as important as setting personal and career goals. By creating SMART (Specific, Measurable, Achievable, Relevant, Time-bound) financial goals, you align your mindset, thoughts, and actions with your desired financial outcomes.

7
Embracing Sustainable Living

Sustainability was a foreign concept to me until I met my husband, Nikhil. He introduced me to the world of sustainable living—full of ideas I never knew existed. All the fascinating concepts and stories he shared with me opened my eyes and helped me see the world through a different lens. As we began implementing some of the sustainable practices, I saw the incredible difference they made in our lives, filling me with contentment and happiness. However, the journey was not without its challenges. Changing our habits and adjusting to a more sustainable lifestyle was difficult. But we persevered, and the rewards were worth it. It's a choice—one we take towards environmental responsibility and our lifestyle. We can blame everyone for not keeping the environment clean and sustainable or start with ourselves.

Sustainable living is about living with minimal waste—reusing, recycling, and reducing waste, thus minimising our contributions to landfills. It's also about being aware of our energy consumption and using it efficiently to consume only what we need, preserving some for the next generation, lowering greenhouse gas emissions, and living in harmony with nature. Being mindful of your contributions and taking a step forward to reduce your carbon footprint are key aspects of sustainability. When you take a step toward sustainable living, you naturally contribute to building a better planet.

Here are some strategies to take a step toward sustainable living. Remember, each small step we take toward sustainable living helps save our planet and restore it as a better place for our children.

Reduce Plastic Consumption

Plastic bags may be banned or restricted in many places, but plastic still infiltrates our daily lives in countless forms. While living completely without plastic may seem impossible, we can take conscious steps to reduce its use. Before purchasing any plastic product or bag, we need to think about its long decomposition time and its devastating impact on pollution. One of the most heartbreaking moments for me was witnessing a wild parrot (a Galah) that visits our backyard daily, entangled in a plastic net. Watching it struggle to fly while dragging the net was a tragic reminder of the consequences of careless waste disposal. This powerful image stays with me and pushes me to act. Every mindful decision to limit plastic consumption can make a significant difference to our planet and protect the wildlife we share it with.

Here are some practical and actionable tips to help you limit plastic consumption in your daily life. These small but meaningful changes can reduce your environmental impact, thus contributing to a cleaner planet.

- Carry a reusable bag with you when shopping. This way, you don't have to buy new plastic bags every time you go shopping. Eventually, it will become a habit for you to take these bags when you go even window shopping.
- Limit the use of disposable items or cutleries by investing in reusable alternatives.
- Encourage the use of biodegradable items instead of plastic items. For instance, when shopping, you can

opt for biodegradable trash bags, compostable cutlery, or even biodegradable packaging materials.

- Promote eco-friendly products and support such local businesses. Many initiatives these days focus on eco-friendly processes and products. Supporting these local businesses and products is a step towards promoting sustainability. Your choice to support eco-friendly products can influence others and contribute to a more significant movement towards sustainability.
- Sort out plastics based on the recycling guidelines mentioned on each product and recycle accordingly. For example, did you know milk cartons have recycling guidelines different from those for yogurt buckets? Understanding these differences can help you maximize the recycling potential of each item.
- Some initiatives collect plastic bottles and containers for free for recycling. Join a recycling community or initiative. It not only helps with recycling but also makes you part of a community working towards a common goal of reducing plastic waste.
- Avoid using plastic bags to pack each vegetable in grocery stores; use paper bags or invest in better eco-friendly alternatives.

Activity: Plastic Audit Challenge

For one week, gather all the plastic items you would normally discard. At the end of the week, categorise them—bottles, wrappers, bags, containers—and take a count. Seeing the volume of plastic waste you generate can be an eye-opener and the first step toward making more sustainable choices. Analyse how many are recyclable and how many are single-use. Also, create an action plan to replace your top 3 most-used plastic items with sustainable alternatives.

Waste Management at Home

For many of us, waste management seems like the last thing on our minds—after all, it's just waste, right? I get it; I felt the same way. But then, I realised how much I was unknowingly adding to landfills and pollution, which changed everything. When I became self-aware of the waste going out of my house, it started making sense; things started looking different. In the old days, our general waste bin was packed every week, and nobody bothered. It was easy to put everything that was no longer needed into the bin. But when we started mindfully disposing of waste and composting vegetable scraps in the backyard, the amount drastically reduced. Some weeks, we don't even need to put the bin outside because there's nothing left to collect. The transition from fully loaded bins to little or no waste is not just impressive; it's deeply satisfying.

Here are some effective and sustainable ways to manage your waste at home, helping you reduce, reuse, and recycle more efficiently.

- Create a compost bin in your backyard. You can start by keeping veggie waste in a separate container, and at the end of the day, you can move it to your compost bin. You will end up mining gold soil from your compost that your plants will love forever.

- If you live in an apartment, you can use an indoor composting system like Bokashi, which you can build yourself using a couple of containers. You would be able to produce rich tea from the compost, which would be a good addition to your plants.
- Use paper and cardboard for composting. Composting requires both green and carbon materials; cardboard and paper packaging are excellent for carbon materials.
- Use lawn clippings from mowing for composting. You can use these clippings for hot composting, as they are rich green materials.
- Engage in DIYs to repurpose household items and furniture. Instead of discarding these items, you can use them for a new project. After painting, we use glass jars as hanging lights, milk containers for planting seedlings, and wood pieces from old furniture for new projects.
- Donate or sell clothes when they are still usable instead of discarding them.
- Move from buying soap and hand washes from attractive packaging to buying in bulk or in refillable bottles.
- Consider using reusable menstrual cups from one-time pads.

From Our Garden: Reused Milk Cartons as Plant Containers

Track your waste and witness the transition from big bags of waste to limited ones. It's not just a transition; it's a journey of joy and motivation.

"When you put the whole picture together, recycling is the right thing to do."

Pam Shoemaker

Growing Your Own Food

Nature never ceases to amaze, and growing your own food brings you one step closer to understanding its magic. Caring for seedlings—watering them, feeding them with natural fertilisers—is like nurturing them into life. While being fully self-sufficient may seem daunting for beginners or intermediate gardeners, you can still strive to grow some of your own food. The sense of accomplishment from sowing a seed, watching it sprout, and harvesting the fruits of your labour is truly magical.

By staying close to nature and planting food, we are helping to reduce food waste by only harvesting what we need. Also, the freshness and taste of the food we produce in our backyard—nothing can beat it. A small veggie garden in your backyard promotes biodiversity and provides a home for beneficial insects, pollinators, and bugs. Knowing you have many companions in your backyard with whom you share your space is a wonderful feeling.

Here are some helpful tips for growing your food, whether you have a backyard or live in an apartment:

- Start with plants suitable to your space and interests. If you are a beginner, start with herbs or easy-growing plants like cucumbers, carrots, and beets. If you live in an apartment, choose container plants that can be placed on your balcony or window. Herbs like mint, coriander, and basil are good starting points.

- Plant a mix of flowers and vegetables to attract beneficial insects. Wildflowers are a good source for attracting bees and butterflies into your garden.
- Prepare your soil by adding a layer of compost and fertilisers. Testing your soil to identify pH levels is also a good idea. Healthy soil is not just a component; it's the foundation for creating a healthy garden.
- Companion planting is a gardening technique in which different species are planted to benefit each other. For instance, planting tomatoes next to basil can help repel pests that are harmful to tomatoes. This way, you can naturally protect your plants without toxic chemicals. Here's a free companion planting guide I created when I first started my veggie garden. Feel free to use it as a starting point.

- If your veggie garden is in a sunny spot, it's beneficial to cover the ground with mulch during summer. Mulch helps to retain moisture in the soil, keeps the soil cool, and suppresses weed growth. This means less watering and weeding for you while raising healthier plants.
- If you live in an apartment, consider growing veggies in LED grow lights. These lights will allow your

plants to receive sufficient light to grow even if your apartment doesn't receive much natural light.
- Watering wisely is essential, no matter where you stay. Depending on the facilities available, you can use sprinklers, drip irrigation, or hand-watering pipes.
- People are moving to vertical gardening, where plants are grown vertically with the help of climbing supports, trellis, etc. This way, you can save a lot of ground space for other plants. Beans, snake beans, pumpkins, melons, and cucumbers are good for vertical gardening.
- Hydroponics is good if you have limited or no space for soil. This method is becoming popular these days and doesn't require soil.
- Having a crop rotation plan is an important step in growing your own food. This reduces the risk of pests and potential diseases. Since each plant requires different nutrients, rotation helps maintain a balanced ecosystem in the soil.

It doesn't matter where you live; you can transform any small space into a beautiful, peaceful place with a mix of flowering and vegetable plants.

Water Conservation Strategies

Water conservation is integral to sustainable living. Conserving water, not only minimizes environmental impact but also reduces your utility costs. The following are some tips for effectively using water in your house and garden.

- Watering early in the morning or late evening could help reduce evaporation compared to afternoons.
- Consider installing a drip irrigation system, as it prevents water evaporation by delivering water directly to the plants' roots.
- Avoid the use of sprinklers, if possible. Instead, opt for water cans or hoses for targeted watering. This simple switch can significantly reduce unnecessary water usage in your garden.
- It is a good idea to install a rainwater harvesting system, such as tanks, containers, or barrels to capture rainwater from the roof. The water collected can be used for watering plants or washing your car, thus reducing reliance on council water.
- By selecting draught-tolerant plants, you can reduce the frequency of watering them as they survive without water. These plants are available as veggies, flowers, and shrubs. Once they are established, they need less water than others.
- Apply mulch on the ground to retain moisture and reduce water evaporation rate.
- Fix leaks in pipes and faucets inside your house immediately. Even a slow drip can waste a significant amount of water over time. You're taking a responsible step towards water conservation by addressing these issues promptly.
- Keeping taps and showers open for a long time consumes a lot of water. Reducing the time spent using taps and showers can save lots of water.

Showering together is also a fun idea if you want to make it fun.

- Graywater recycling from washrooms, washing machines, and dishes can save water and be used in your garden.
- When you wash vegetables or lentils, instead of discarding the water in the basin, collect it and use it to water your plants at the end of the day. This starch and nutrient-rich water is beneficial for plants, as it provides them with an additional boost.

Sustainable Energy Use

Sustainable energy use is about reducing dependence on nonrenewable energy while making conscious choices to limit environmental impact. Shifting from nonrenewable sources to renewable energy sources like solar and wind is a perfect place to start.

You can lower your carbon footprint by shifting to more sustainable energy sources, paving the way for a brighter, more sustainable future. It's about understanding and applying a balance between energy utilisation and environmental stewardship.

Here are some simple and practical ways to use energy sustainably.

- Select appliances with the highest energy efficiency rating. This way, you can lower energy consumption while promoting sustainability.

- Replace traditional light bulbs with LED lights. This is a small yet important step toward energy conservation. LED lights consume significantly less energy compared to traditional bulbs, thus contributing to a more sustainable energy use.
- Be mindful when you switch on the air conditioner or heating; this awareness can sometimes save hours of energy consumption. Setting a timer on these appliances to automatically switch off after some time is also a good idea.
- Wear proper clothing during winter instead of turning on heaters 24/7; thus, you can avoid switching on heaters to an extent.
- Practice turning off lights and electronic items when not in use. If you charge your phone at night until dawn, maybe consider switching it off once it's fully charged or change your charging time to avoid using energy unnecessarily.
- Use motion-censored lights in areas with limited motion in your house.
- Consider investing in electric or hybrid vehicles to limit reliance on fossil fuels.
- Use energy-efficient curtains with insulated fabric to block the exchange of heat and light. This will reduce heat gain in summer and heat loss in winter.
- Install solar panels to use the sun's energy for electricity needs.
- Consider small wind turbines for additional energy if you have a big backyard.

"Sustainability is no longer about doing less harm. It's about doing more good."

Jochen Zeitz

Activity: Home Energy Audit

Conduct a simple home energy audit in your house. List out 5 energy-efficient improvements you could introduce to save energy.

1.

___

2.

___

3.

___

4.

___

5.

___

Assessing your energy consumption will help you understand where to reduce your impact on the environment, taking one step toward sustainable living.

Key Points to Remember

- Sustainable living is about living with minimal waste—reusing, recycling, and reducing waste, thus minimising our contributions to landfills.
- Being aware of our energy consumption and using it efficiently to consume only what we need, preserving some for the next generation, lowering greenhouse gas emissions, and living in harmony with nature are small steps toward sustainability.
- Every mindful action we take to limit plastic waste makes a huge difference. No effort is too small.
- Think about creating a compost bin in your backyard. If you live in an apartment, you can use an indoor composting system like Bokashi. This way, you can reduce the waste being sent to landfil while mining gold soil from your compost.
- Growing your own food, even on a small scale, brings a deeper connection to nature.
- Water is an essential resource that we need to preserve. Small actions like fixing leaks, turning off the tap when not in use, and being mindful of your shower time are simple steps you can implement immediately.
- Being mindful of your energy usage and making conscious efforts to limit it is a responsibility we should all embrace.

8

Turning Miles into Memories

Travel offers unique experiences—for some, it's an opportunity to unwind and enjoy holidays; for others, it's a chance to learn a new skill or engage in various adventurous activities. The purpose of travel can vary for different people at different times; there's no one-size-fits-all approach. For example, you might visit New Zealand to admire its stunning landscapes on a relaxing trip, Bali to immerse yourself in its vibrant culture, or India to learn yoga. Every country has its own unique stories and rich culture to share. Staying open to various travel experiences broadens your perspective and helps you discover a sense of purpose behind your journeys. It's about stepping into a world of new possibilities and fostering an open-minded and curious approach to travel.

Travel often reminds me of the things I may have forgotten on life's journey—memories shared with loved ones, the blessings I often overlook, or simple reflections on my life. But each return from a trip leaves me feeling invigorated and with a clearer vision of the changes I want to make in my life. Road trips, particularly with the wind in your hair and a sense of rawness, inspire deep reflection and personal growth.

From my background, I used to think that travel meant covering all the places in that country and exploring every corner. But now, I realise it doesn't need to be that way. It could be just visiting a part of a country, relaxing in your way and having a good time. For me, it's no more exploring places; it's the memories I make, the reflections, and a break from our busy schedules while exploring some stories that unfold. Again, it may or may not resonate with you as it can differ from person to person and change from time to time. What I found from travel a few years ago, I can no longer resonate with it. My intentions and purpose of travel also grow and change as I grow. Understanding what travel means to you will give you more clarity and a sense of purpose.

Planning Trips with Purpose

When planning a trip, most people start by choosing the destination and then deciding on activities and sightseeing spots. Here's another approach to try occasionally: start by setting an intention or purpose for your trip. For instance, if you want to experience a white Christmas or try adrenaline-filled activities like cave exploring or bungee jumping, let that purpose guide your destination choice. This way, your travel aligns with your goals. I'm not suggesting you always start with an intention, but it's an alternative way to think about the travel planning process.

I often find that setting an intention helps narrow down the travel destination and organise the trip. Having this intention makes the journey more fulfilling and creates meaningful memories. Just remember, travel doesn't always need to involve ticking off must-see places; it's more about reflecting on your values and embracing a journey that shapes your life.

The following are some travel inspirations you can choose from for your travel plans.

- Explore the culture of a country
- Experience an adventure activity like a hot air balloon or skydiving

- Learn a new skill like surfing, skiing, or diving
- Learn and practice yoga
- Experience the beauty of nature, whether it be mountains, oceans, or deserts
- Enjoy a relaxed vacation from hustles and reflect
- Visit your family and restore connections
- Participate in volunteering and contribute to communities
- A solo trip to know you better
- Trip with friends and embrace the child within you
- Experience snowy winter
- Hiking or Trekking
- Experience wildlife (safaris or marine wildlife)
- Spiritual growth, such as healing and meditation

You could always combine more than one goals in just one travel trip—like hiking, learning a skill, and a solo trip or having a relaxed vacation while experiencing the beauty of nature. Ultimately, you should feel refreshed and relaxed when you come back from a trip rather than exhausted. If the latter is you, it may be time to think and adjust your travel.

Travel planners

Travel planners are not just for planning your trip but also a treasure trove of memories. These organisers are designed to help you plan your trip, organise, and travel without missing any essential details. With dedicated space for your itinerary, packing list, travel budget, and more, travel planners keep all your trip information in one convenient place. And the best part? Looking back after many years, you'll find all the information and good memories of your travels in the planner. It's a wonderful way to relive your adventures and get excited about future trips!

If you're looking for a travel planner, scan the QR code below to check it out on Amazon and see how it works.

Activity: Travel Vision Board

Create a digital or physical vision board of your dream destinations and experiences. Use photos, text, drawings, or any form of art to bring your vision to life and add a personal, magical touch.

"One day your life will flash before your eyes, make sure it's worth watching."

Gerard Way

Balancing Local, Domestic, and International Travel

Travel doesn't always need to be international; it can involve local exploration or domestic trips. Balancing these three can create a great experience. By exploring places locally, you can enjoy nearby treasures and hidden gems. Traveling locally or within your country also supports local tourism and businesses. While local and domestic travel offers these benefits, international travel provides an opportunity to understand different cultures, people, and lifestyles, expanding your worldview.

Exploring your own country

There are countless ways to explore your state or country. Here are some ideas to inspire your next adventure.

- If you like to go for a trail walk, explore a farmer's market in an area, or even attend any unique events in a town, start there.
- Book a Staycation in a hotel or Airbnb in your town and enjoy the getaway. This helps you get a fresh perspective and a break from daily chores while still staying in your town.
- Camping is a fantastic way to explore places. It offers a serene escape from the hustle and bustle of daily life. Whether you're a nature lover or simply seeking a peaceful retreat, a night under the stars promises a refreshing experience and the opportunity to create lasting memories.

- Explore national parks with your friends or family and have a picnic surrounded by trees.
- Take advantage of seasonal events, such as fringe festivals, cherry blossom festivals, or pumpkin harvest festivals, that are popular in your town. Book a B&B and enjoy the festival to the fullest. Alternatively, make a day trip!
- Create a list on social media based on the country or state. For instance, when I come across posts or reels related to say Tasmania, I save them to a 'Tasmania' list I created on social media. This way, I can easily access it whenever I am in the mood to explore places, without wasting time searching.

Planning for international trip

When you plan your international trip, the following are some of the things I suggest doing:

- Research the country—its culture, attractions, cost, specialities, alerts, etc. You can do this by reading travel blogs, watching documentaries, or contacting locals on social media. This way, you can be prepared by knowing what to expect and what to be careful of.
- Decide your budget and start planning accordingly. We allocate an amount for each category, such as renting a car, stay, food, flights, miscellaneous items, etc. This way, we can understand our travel expenses and plan wisely.
- If you book your flight tickets early enough, you will save some money compared to last-minute bookings. However, ticket prices vary greatly by country. It may

not be wise to book a ticket to Europe at the last minute, but a ticket to a closer country could be affordable. Do your research and book accordingly.

- Booking your flight tickets on a Tuesday or Wednesday might be the best time, according to some travel enthusiasts. Be sure to do your research and find the best deals.
- If you are fine with off-season traveling, you will find lower prices for accommodation and activities. You can save a lot this way. We visited New Zealand during winter and were able to get a campervan for a cheaper price compared to peak season. You can decide on this based on your circumstances and situation.
- Try to travel on Tuesdays or Wednesdays as the airports will be less crowded, and you can travel peacefully.
- Travel and health insurance are a must if you travel globally. They can protect you in case something unexpected happens and give you tremendous peace of mind.
- Currency exchange is something that you need to consider before your travels. You can do it online through currency conversion apps like Wise or in the country you plan to visit.
- Beware of theft or any such activities in the country or area you plan to visit. Being aware will help you avoid such situations and regrets. Dressing as a local rather than a tourist often helps avoid unnecessary attractions from other people.

- Research about economical and convenient travel modes in the country.
- If you are making bookings for stays and activities, I recommend checking for refundable bookings. This way, if you are stuck for any unforeseen reason, you can reschedule your trip.
- When traveling, being mindful of your impact on the destination is crucial. Opt for eco-friendly accommodations, support local businesses, and contribute to the sustainability of the community you're visiting.

If you want to travel but are unsure where and how to start, I recommend starting by setting your travel intention. This way, you figure out what travel experiences you're after. Then, allocate a budget against the travel. Once you allocate a budget, you can explore your options and finalise a country of travel based on your interests and goals. Once this is done, I highly recommend booking your flights or making some bookings for your travel plan. This way, you are committing to your travel and travel savings. Most of us want to travel, but it doesn't get to the execution phase as we often fall behind in money, resources, or annual leave. By booking flights or stays in the form of a commitment, you have already started the execution phase and mostly end up traveling. By exploring the local towns and the world around you, you can gain a lifetime of enriching experiences and a new perspective.

Taking a Sabbatical

A sabbatical is an intentional break from daily routines, allowing time for exploration, self-development, or rejuvenation. It's a planned pause from work or regular commitments, typically lasting a few months to a year. Whether you want to develop a new skill, explore a country by road, or recharge yourself, a well-planned sabbatical can be a life changer. You can take a sabbatical when you work continuously for some years; some say 5 years, and others 7 years. Listen to your body and mind—they know what's best for you!

Sabbaticals offer many benefits, such as time for self-reflection, recharge, and restoration. It helps one to learn new skills and view things from different perspectives. It challenges you in many ways, often pushing you out of your comfort zone and bringing new ideas and changes that drive transformation.

When you plan for your sabbatical, you can plan with a variety of activities, such as travel, volunteering, learning, and more—it doesn't have to be just one thing. For instance, we plan to travel across some European countries, take a laid-back countryside road trip, and have many chitchats while immersing ourselves in nature's beauty. This will not only be a relaxing experience but also a chance to learn about different cultures and lifestyles. We also plan to build a DIY Koi Pond in our backyard, which will be a hands-on learning experience. And lastly, we want to go on a solo trip to learn a new skill like diving or healing, which will be a personal growth journey. This sabbatical break is something that drives us during difficult situations. It feels so exciting to take a break from 9-5 work and live our dreams.

A successful sabbatical requires careful planning and budgeting to ensure you can make the most of your time away without financial stress. This means considering all potential expenses, from travel and accommodation to insurance and home maintenance.

Here are some high-level steps you can take to ensure your sabbatical is well planned and financially secure:

- Define your purpose: Decide what you want to achieve from the sabbatical and choose your destinations accordingly. Consider how long you want to take your break based on your purpose.
- Decide on your budget for the sabbatical. If you are planning a long sabbatical break, you may need to prepare for a large budget. It would help if you considered your travel expenses, accommodations for the duration of the sabbatical, insurance, and other activities. You may also need to consider your monthly mortgages and other household expenses as you may need to continue paying them even though you are away. I would suggest keeping a safety deposit, excluding the Sabbatical amount, just for emergencies.
- Create a savings plan based on your income and start saving accordingly. Cut down on expenses, set up auto transfers from your main account to your savings account, and look for more budget-friendly options.

- Plan your travel logistics, such as visa, passport (check passport expiry), vaccinations, and insurance.
- Draft your route and an itinerary as soon as you can. It may consume more of your time and energy and might require several revisions.
- Prepare household and work-related tasks, such as booking annual leave or planning a career break, setting up automatic utility bill payments, arranging for someone to check on your house, and delegating tasks to avoid last-minute stress and ensure a smooth transition. If you're concerned about work commitments, discuss a potential sabbatical with your employer well in advance. This will help you plan effectively and ensure your responsibilities are managed in your absence.

It may sound easy, but from my experience, it requires at least 6-8 months of planning and preparation. So, brace yourself!

"Do not go where the path may lead, go instead where there is no path and leave a trail."

Ralph Waldo Emerson

Incorporating Travel Into Your Lifestyle

With remote work becoming more popular worldwide, travel is becoming more straightforward. Many professionals combine work and travel with modern technology while maintaining their professional lives. Finding a remote work role would be a good idea if you are keen to travel continuously. Employers are flexible and stay open these days to ensure employees have a flexible work environment and better work-life balance.

When you choose your travel destination and accommodations, ensure they have a stable internet connection and work desk space so that you can work without interruption during the travel. If your employer doesn't promote remote work arrangements, you can still try to make the most out of your annual leave and public holidays. For this, plan your trips around public holidays well in advance. This will enable you to avoid peak time rates. If you can, try to travel during off-peak season. This way, take advantage of less crowded and more affordable travel packages.

Incorporating travel into your life doesn't mean you need to sacrifice your work. With the right strategies and planning, you can have a balance between your travel plans and work life.

Activity: Travel Integration Roadmap

Create a 6-12-month calendar, marking potential travel opportunities and how they fit with your work/life commitments.

Capture and Preserve Travel Memories

When I return from a trip, I never miss the opportunity to preserve travel memories—whether it's creating a photo album, collecting unique souvenirs that tell a story, or journalling my experiences. These memories are truly priceless. And when you revisit them years later, they'll bring back a flood of beautiful, nostalgic feelings.

If the idea of a travel journal entices you, you can start it as soon as you begin planning your trip. You can include your travel itinerary, goals, experiences, and emotions within your journal. It reflects your unique travel experience from the moment you start planning to the end of your journey. You can add photos, ticket stubs, postcards, or maps - there are no strict rules, just the freedom to journal as you like.

If you enjoy revisiting your travel experiences through photographs, that's wonderful. You can create a physical travel album with selected photos or store digital copies on your laptop, in the cloud, or on a hard disk. I personally do both—I print out our photos in a book each year and display them in our living room. On a rainy day, we sit with a cup of tea and relive these beautiful moments. It's a joy to share these memories with loved ones. Alternatively, if you want a souvenir collection, you can purchase one from every country you visit. It could be anything from small artwork to magnets to postcards.

Preserving your travel memories can be a way to reflect on the experiences you've had and the places you've been. The memories you have today will become treasures you'll carry with you forever.

Key Points to Remember

- Staying open to various travel experiences broadens your perspective. It also allows you to connect with different cultures and viewpoints.
- Identify the purpose of your trip and set an intention. This will help you plan better and ensure a fulfilling travel experience that lasts.
- A balance between local, domestic, and international travel offers a wide variety of experiences and exposure.
- A sabbatical is a break from something you've been doing continuously for a long time. It's recommended to consider taking a sabbatical every 5-7 years.
- Preserving memories from travel can be a treasure that brings a smile when time passes. These memories are truly priceless. When you revisit them years later, they'll bring back a flood of beautiful, nostalgic feelings.

9

Building Stronger and Healthier Relationships

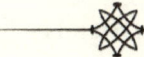

Cultivate Friendships

One of life's greatest treasures is a beautiful friendship, a bond that feels like family. The unwavering support, laughter, love, and companionship it offers are nothing short of magical. It fills the spaces we never knew were empty. When life feels heavy, a simple chat with a friend can lift your spirit. Friends are like mirrors—reflecting the best in you, supporting you when you need it most, and encouraging your growth. In true friendship, there is no judgment, only a safe space to be yourself—blunt, silly, and completely authentic.

Some are lucky to find genuine friendships from a young age; others build them along the way. Appreciating friendships and actively nurturing them is the secret recipe to strengthening and continuing the bond. It could be as simple as calling your friends occasionally, visiting them, organising catch-ups and sleepovers, going on trips or camping—whatever aligns with the spirit of your friendship. I am blessed with friends who feel like family—those who stand by me through my highs and lows, even crossing great distances to be with me when I need them the most. They are close to my heart and always will be.

Like in relationships, expressing love and affection is equally important in friendships, tailored to the unique bond you share. Some friendships are very expressive, speaking regularly and hanging out often to show their love and care, while others are just the opposite. For example, if your friend is not very expressive, you can show your love by being there for them in times of need or doing something thoughtful for them. Understanding the language of your friendship is necessary to strengthen the bond and communicate better.

A good friend always remain honest and speaks the truth, even when it's hard to hear. They share it with the intention of helping the other person grow and improve. True friends are willing to engage in difficult conversations, pointing out flaws when necessary, while providing a shoulder to lean on in times of need. Without the unwavering support of true friends, I wouldn't be the person I am today. Cheers to all the amazing friends who make life better!

Let's explore how one can nurture a friendship meaningfully. Some friendships thrive on shared adventures, like traveling or hanging out, while others flourish through simple, thoughtful gestures. Regardless of the dynamic of your friendship and no matter how busy life gets, staying connected is essential. Plan day trips, try out fun activities together, or simply be present in their lives. Surprise them with heartfelt gifts, photographs, or handwritten letters when they least expect it. Personally, I enjoy writing letters or crafting something meaningful—it's a time investment that reminds both me and my friend of the value of our bond. Also, remembering birthdays and special dates can mean the world to your friends, especially if they cherish such gestures. Save these dates on your calendar with reminders so you don't miss them. Often, these small, thoughtful actions create a lasting impact, showing your friends how much they mean to you.

Activity: Reconnect With Your Friends

Think of a friend you haven't reached out to in a while. Plan a catch-up or a thoughtful gesture to reconnect with them. It could be as simple as a heartfelt message, a quick call, or even a surprise action like sending a small gift or a handwritten note. These little things matter more than you realise and can strengthen your bond.

Maintain a Healthy Romantic Relationship

This is one of my favourite topics in this book, and I love sharing its insights the most. A romantic relationship—whether as girlfriend and boyfriend or husband and wife—is magical yet hard to describe in words. It is built on love, trust, honesty, care, and commitment. The foundation of a healthy romantic relationship must always be strong so that, no matter the storms they face, they can return to peaceful nights quickly because their bond is unbreakable.

How does one build such a strong, healthy relationship with their partner? Firstly, foster open communication. Often, we underestimate the power of open communication, but it can do wonders. Whether you are in disagreement, a conflicting situation, or a fight, communicate openly. This will help you understand each other's perspective and determine where this issue stems. Secondly, do not hesitate to be expressive. Share with your partner how you feel about a particular situation: anxiety, sadness, happiness, or gratitude. We often hope our partner will do certain things to make us happy, but how can they know what brings you joy if you don't express it clearly?

Another point to reflect on is how often you embrace honest and transparent conversations with your partner. Having honest discussions during your personal space is key to building a healthy relationship. Discuss your dreams, aspirations, weaknesses, and vulnerabilities with your partner. This will help build intimacy and show them that you trust your partner. Besides, celebrate small wins to make your relationship unique and memorable. These moments of celebration are not just about the win but about acknowledging the effort and commitment that went into achieving it. You can also celebrate your failures with your partner as a symbol of continuous learning during hard times.

Now, let's look at how you can handle disagreements in a way that strengthens your bond. When you discuss conflicting topics and disagreements, discuss them privately instead of in front of family or public. This will help you be yourself in such open conversation without the pressure of censoring or altering your words in a public setting, fostering a more genuine and honest conversation. It is also crucial not to bring up past arguments to win a current disagreement. Doing so goes against your inner values and won't contribute positively to the growth of your relationship. Also, do not hesitate to apologise when you're wrong. Apologising makes one grounded, and it removes unwanted ego from a relationship. My husband and I always apologise to each other after every fight, even if one of us isn't entirely at fault. We believe that just like the sound of two hands clapping, both of us contribute to the situation. There's always something the other person could've done to make it better, even if it's just 1% of the issue. In lighter moments, we sometimes make each other do squats with our hands crossed over our ears, turning a tense moment into something playful and helping us move past the fight quickly. You can also try resolving any issues or disagreements with your partner before going to bed. This way, you will not channel unwanted energy into a precious relationship. Lastly, you can reflect on the incident together once the weather has been cleared. You can consider discussing how to avoid similar situations in the future, what hurt you, what should be avoided, how you could have communicated it better without hurting, etc. This is very powerful, especially if you do it right after you solve the problem between you both.

Compromising can often be seen as challenging, especially when your partner and you are in two different places, like the north and south poles. In such cases, I suggest finding a middle ground. If both of you are willing to compromise what you can, you will reach the middle ground or at least be closer to the middle ground. To achieve this, you need to embrace a flexible and open mindset. When you genuinely compromise or give up something with an open heart, your partner will undoubtedly feel and appreciate it. This act speaks volumes, as it shows through your actions just how much the other person means to you. Show appreciation for small efforts from your partner's side, especially if they are making efforts to make you happy. Sometimes, a tight hug or thoughtful actions like buying flowers or preparing your partner's favorite food could take you a long way.

Another fascinating thing I've noticed is that at the beginning of a relationship, you might say "I love you" a hundred times. But as time passes, say, after five years, how often do you say it? It's such a powerful phrase; by saying it, you remind yourself and your partner of the love and commitment you share. So, if you feel that the frequency has dropped, make an effort to say it more often and with genuine feelings to keep that connection alive and strong. It will make a significant impact on your relationship. I am not suggesting you practice saying "I love you" if you are uncomfortable. It could be any thoughtful action you used to do in the beginning phase that has faded or disappeared—that one thing can be reintroduced to your relationship if it adds value. It's more about embracing things we once valued and still value but miss during our busy lives. Small acts like seeing off your partner or welcoming them home after work can truly strengthen your bond and bring a smile to their face. Similarly, adding a warm hug before they leave for work or as they return home creates a special, heartfelt connection that reinforces your affection for one another. These little things are super important to me, and I do it with lots of affection and love towards him. Another simple thing you could consider is spending time after work to know their day. Having these little conversations makes a massive difference in your relationship. This will bring a sense of care and closeness, strengthening the bond over time.

Bringing fun elements is essential for maintaining balance and a thriving relationship. Fun could be different for different couples, such as introducing date nights, candlelight dinners, thoughtful surprises, outdoor couple activities, or simply spending time together in a good ambience. Incorporating these elements is necessary to know each other better and build a stronger connection. Going on trips together helps to have open conversations and gain new perspectives. We often feel refreshed after a road trip as we have spoken about everything under the stars during the drive, and our minds would be like a clean slate.

Counselling is another way to improve any relationship. Even if everything is going well, visit a relationship counsellor and find something to improve, which will come in handy. By seeking counselling, you are not admitting defeat but showing that you value your relationship enough to seek professional help. Counselling is often seen as a service for people who need some support in their lives. In my opinion, it is not so. After consulting with a counsellor, we got new perspectives, which helped us understand ourselves even more from a different lens. We never miss a chance to improve our relationship because that's something we value the most!

Lastly, I want to highlight continuous efforts. During the journey, you might find that the things you once enjoyed no longer bring you the same joy. Your shared interests would have changed eventually. This could happen at any point in time as you outgrow. For instance, if you and your partner used to love playing chess but you now start feeling slightly off about it, an open conversation is essential. This allows your partner to understand how and why your feelings have changed. There's nothing to worry about—both of you may simply need to discover the next activity you enjoy together. Your interests won't always remain the same throughout your journey. But as they evolve, it's important to prioritise open and transparent communication and continue investing in your relationship.

Relationships can be a beautiful gift when nurtured with love, affection, care, and other meaningful actions.

Nurturing Family Connections

Family is where you can truly be yourself, and there's always a seat reserved for you, no matter how busy the place is. It is the building block of our lives, providing warmth, love, support, and a sense of belonging. In a family, you don't need to wear a mask; you can express your feelings, emotions, and opinions without fear of judgment. One of the greatest blessings in my life is my family—being there for me and offering a place to turn to, even at midnight when I feel low. But how do you build such deep family connections? How do you nurture them with love and compassion? That's where the secret lies.

Maintaining a strong family connection requires lots of effort, and every member of your family has to nurture it. If only one person makes an effort to build family connections, it doesn't work that way. We may need to build a family that values the following:

- Trust and Honesty: Building trust is important in every relationship, and family is no different. Having a trusted environment helps one open up and feel secure. Honesty is part of it, as you can't build trust without being honest. When I ask my family for advice on big decisions, I know I can trust their opinions, as they will always be honest with me. This is an essential factor when you build your family.

- Respect: Valuing and respecting every member of the family equally is important, too. It doesn't matter if it is your kid or grandparent—it applies to everyone equally. Acknowledging every member's opinions and decisions without being judgmental and respecting their individuality is crucial. For instance, respecting your child's decision to pursue a particular course or your grandparent's desire to share their life experiences can strengthen family bonds. I believe firmly in give-and-take respect.

- Open communication: It is super important to have open and transparent communication in your family. Hiding something from others and keeping secrets unnecessarily do not promote a healthy relationship or family. Any problem can be resolved by encouraging open communication and respect for everyone.

- Commitment: You need to stay committed to your family—no matter how busy your schedule is. Make family your priority and find time for it. Be committed to standing by your family through thick and thin.

- Empathy: Empathy and understanding the emotions of others without judging them are necessary for a healthy family. Put yourself in others' shoes, which will help you understand what they are going through.

Be with them by listening to their story, sharing your experience, or simply holding their hands.
- Forgiveness: When you forgive someone, you release all the negative emotions that you were holding closer to your heart. You let go of the resentments and grudges. This helps resolve any conflict or difficult conversation in any environment by simply realising that everybody makes mistakes, including ourselves.

If you struggle to carve out time for your family, apply strategies like dedicating a specific time in your day or week for them. I often speak to my sisters on Saturday mornings right after my morning routine, and we spend hours talking and sharing. It has become a habit for me to talk to them during my weekends. Similarly, I talk to my parents every evening right after work. This has become an automatic action from my end as I have combined these calls with an action I do without effort. Another way to spend time with family is to engage in activities like cooking meals together, doing picnics every fortnightly, or going for walks together. If you are staying away from your family, determine your visiting frequency and keep those days fixed when planning your holiday or events. Ultimately, sharing little stories, laughing, being there for one another, and supporting them when needed are part of the journey. These moments of togetherness are what make life truly beautiful and worth living.

Effective communication is one of the pillars of a happy and healthy family. Being open and transparent is important, giving one a sense of togetherness. I feel most issues that evolve in a house can be resolved by fostering open communication. It is a cornerstone of any relationship. If you aren't open about your feelings, how can others understand why you responded in a particular way? If you keep concerns or resentment in your mind for a long time, it accumulates, and you blow out one day. This is quite severe compared to taking the courage to express how you feel at that moment. It's gone once you share it, and you feel instantly relieved. Otherwise, you carry a bag full of burdens, knowingly or unknowingly.

Another aspect of open communication is being a good listener. Not always does one need to speak and resolve issues. Sometimes, we need to be a good listener. Analysing the situation and acting accordingly is essential. The relief from sharing your feelings openly is unparalleled, strengthening the bond within the family. When I talk to my mom, my role is usually to be a good listener. When she needs an opinion, she asks for it. If you listen carefully, you will understand the difference. This will help you talk when required rather than jumping into everything and having your say.

Lastly, I want to highlight emotional baggage. By emotional baggage, I mean an action or inaction by yourself or someone else in the past that caused you pain or frustration. Often, you end up in a conversation pointing to the past and blaming someone for what they did. How does it help? Do you think the person being accused will listen and sincerely apologise? It will only intensify both of your arguments or frustrations. Instead of holding on to emotional baggage, address it openly so that you don't have to refer to it occasionally.

"Honest, open communication is the only street that leads us into the real world. Communication works for those who work at it."

John Powell

If you have a lot of trumps or frustrations in your mind, list them and write down the person involved in them. Have an open conversation with that person if the situation permits. Ensure you are gentle, honest, and polite while expressing your feelings. You would be blown away by the weight you release from your heart. This particular incident will never trigger in your mind when a similar incident happens, and you will never point to this past incident again because that's done and dusted for you. For instance, I often hear couples saying to their partners, *"You harassed me in front of everyone, and I felt humiliated."* If you don't open up, this will never help you except for holding a grudge in every following action. Instead of keeping it in your mind, have an open conversation with your partner about how you feel about their actions. This way, they might understand you and try never to repeat it. That open conversation will help remove that black mark from your mind, and both of you will move forward happily.

Another example is when your in-laws visit, and you don't like something they do. Instead of keeping it to yourself and suppressing it, openly communicate with them. Have a genuine conversation, as people can usually distinguish between genuine and non-genuine interactions. Most of the time, you'll either understand why they are doing it, or they will stop doing it. Either way, you'll better understand each other and move forward with a lighter heart.

When it comes to family, our parents play a huge role, from raising us from babies to fully grown adults. Whatever we do, nothing is enough to keep up with their selfless love and care for us. There are many things that we can do for them, including the following:

- Spend quality time with your parents.
- Acknowledge their efforts and selfless love and appreciate it whenever you can.
- Motivate them to do what they have been doing until now—engaging in community activities, going for walks, and learning something new. When parents get older, they tend to be less social. Always encourage them to do what they love and be there to support them.
- Sometimes, we feel like they don't understand modern or fancy things at our age, and we try not to bother explaining things to them or ignore them by answering vaguely. Is that what they did to us when we were kids? How hard they tried to explain things to us repeatedly. At least if we could give 1% of it back, they would be so happy.
- Care for them as much as possible without expecting anything. When we were dependent, they selflessly cared for us without any complaints and with an open heart full of joy. It is an opportunity for us to care for them when they need us. Do not see that as a responsibility. When it becomes a responsibility, it becomes a task we don't do with love.
- If their health permits, go on trips with them. Help them do things that they thought they couldn't do again.
- Cherish moments with them—whether it is past or present. It could be by discussing a moment you had with your parents at a younger age or a fun time or any such sort.

- Sometimes, small actions, like talking to them over the phone or in person, taking them out for dinner, or buying them gifts, make a huge difference in their world. And we lose nothing in return.

Activity: Family Connection Calendar

Create a monthly calendar with planned family activities and one-on-one time with each family member. I'm pretty sure you'll surprisingly find a gap, a realisation that you haven't contacted someone in a while, or you may have wanted to but didn't get the time.

Unplug to Reconnect

Relationships are often put in the backseat when everybody moves towards technology. We fail to value and prioritise relationships in front of technology. Scrolling through their phone or laptop while conversing with family or friends has become a norm. We reached a state of mind where nothing is unusual about using social media while having a family dinner or to watch reels while spending time with our children. We used to smile at people while walking along the pathway, but now, no one seems to have time for that—most are either talking on the phone or engaged in something on their screen. This has become the reality. Exchanging smiles when walking past strangers on the road, engaging in a conversation without digital interruption, enjoying a meal without notification from your phone, and sleeping without looking at the phone are gone forever. We may find ourselves physically present over many meaningful discussions but emotionally distant.

How do you feel when you ask someone a question and they answer you with the least importance, checking their phone multiple times and giving a broken response? Do you think you are important to that person? Do you feel like continuing that conversation? No. It's as simple as that. I believe relationships are something that is most impacted by digital disruptions.

Unplug to reconnect is about breaking this pattern through conscious efforts and awareness. It is about stepping away from screens and providing undivided attention to people you interact with. This way, you enrich your relationships and give them importance. By actively listening and responding, you show that you value the people in your life. You open the door to meaningful conversations with your family and friends, sharing and valuing experiences and engaging in emotions and feelings. Sharing your feelings openly with others helps foster stronger connections. By doing so, you encourage the other person to reciprocate with similar actions and emotions, creating a mutual understanding. Committing to this practice allows you to embrace a healthier relationship while creating authentic and meaningful memories.

The art of deep listening

Often, we're eager to share our thoughts and ideas, sometimes at the expense of truly hearing what the other person has to say. But is this the best way to communicate? Not really! Effective listening is a cornerstone of healthy relationships.

Here are some practical steps you can take to enhance your listening skills, and the benefits are worth it.

- Your physical body language speaks a lot more than you think. Maintaining an open and relaxed posture, such as not crossing your hands or putting them in your pockets, signals that you are comfortable and open to the conversation. This can help the speaker feel more at ease and encourage them to share more openly.
- Be present by removing any distractions from you, such as mobile phones, and focus on the speaker.
- Wait patiently for the speaker to finish before you share your thoughts or ask questions.
- Try not to be judgmental. Let them finish and show patience while listening to them completely.
- Ask any follow-up questions, if applicable.
- Do not worry about your response. Let it flow automatically.
- It is a good idea to remember what they mentioned last week and ask about it next week. This shows that you value the conversation and are interested in their life. For instance, if they mentioned they were going fishing, you could ask how the fishing trip went, what they caught, or if they enjoyed the experience. This shows active listening and interest in their story.
- Practice patience. People can take a long time to express themselves. Having patience is the key, rather than rushing them or interrupting them.

"The biggest communication problem is we do not listen to understand; we listen to reply."

Stephen R. Covey

Other Thoughts

- Before getting caught up in toxic arguments, consider the consequences. How do you feel after the argument? Do you feel content and at peace? I do not mean to suppress your feelings; instead, empower yourself with open communication. It's a powerful tool that can steer your relationships in a positive direction.
- Relationships are continuous efforts. They need our time and effort; they will start to droop if you stop feeding them. They are not something that will grow and nurture automatically. Like plants need water and food, relationships need their nutrient-rich intake.
- Take time to analyse every relationship. Do you want to improve your relationship with someone? If so, how and what steps can you take? Do you want to get rid of any toxic relationships in your life? Reflecting on this will allow you to audit your life and how these relationships affect you positively and negatively.
- Appreciation and gratitude are essential. Often, we take relationships for granted and fail to focus on the good. Expressing gratitude will help you understand how much these relationships mean to you and the value they add to your life.
- Giving each other space is also essential. It is important to give them the freedom to pursue what they enjoy and the autonomy to avoid what they don't. Imagining how you would feel when the other person is so restrictive to you will help you understand better.

- I am a big fan of surprises. Who doesn't like some exciting moments in their lives? It can be booking a ticket to a cinema, gifting a surfing lesson, buying a cute notebook, or anything simple! Remember, it is also the other person's responsibility to appreciate the gift without looking at the size or price tag; instead, look at the person's efforts and time.
- The efforts we make at different stages of life are not the same. It is important to understand that these efforts evolve over time. For instance, the energy and attention I dedicated to our relationship in its early stages are different from the efforts I make now.
- We have been practicing mutual responsibility since the beginning. For any tasks or decisions in our lives, we both take equal responsibility and put in effort without leaving everything to one person. This way, I feel we are connected in everything we do, and we get to support each other while getting the best out of everything.

Looking back at my life, I realise that relationships—including those with my family, friends, and husband—are the true wealth I cherish deeply. They bring immense joy and fulfilment to my life. However, relationships are fragile; it requires continuous care, effort, and understanding to thrive. Just like a garden, they need nurturing, attention, and love to flourish. If you feed them with love and respect, you can build a heaven to live in.

Key Points to Remember

- True friendships are built on trust, honesty, and mutual support. Appreciating friendships and actively nurturing them is the secret recipe to strengthening and continuing the bond.
- A successful relationship blooms when you put in constant effort, encourage open communication, and regularly express love, gratitude, and appreciation. Making an effort to know each other's feelings and having honest and transparent conversations can significantly strengthen the bond.
- Family is the foundation of our lives, offering unconditional love, support, and a safe space to be our true selves. Building deep family connections requires nurturing them with love, compassion, and understanding.
- Strengthen relationships by stepping away from screens and giving undivided attention to your loved ones. Engage in meaningful conversations, openly communicate expectations, and nurture mutual understanding to build healthier, authentic connections and create lasting memories.

Tools and Resources

Resources	QR code
Gratitude Journal: My Daily Dose of Joy	
Bucket List	
Mortgage Pay-off Tracker	

Travel Planner: Roam & Record	
Enchanted Candles (Pure Soy Candles)	
The Urban Growers Youtube Channel for Gardening	

The Power of Daily Habit: Free Trackers	
Mindful Living: Free Affirmations	
Harmonious Home: Free Declutter Template	

Wealth Mindset: Free Mortgage Payoff Tracker	
Sustainable Living: Free Companion Planting Guide	

www.ingramcontent.com/pod-product-compliance
Lightning Source LLC
Chambersburg PA
CBHW060559080526
44585CB00013B/625